2024
Ladies
Devotional Book

FREED-HARDEMAN
BIBLE LECTURESHIP

Published by FHU Press
fhu.edu

Editor: Doug Burleson

Cover Design: Bramblett Group
Interior Layout: Joey Sparks

They will make war on the Lamb, and the Lamb will conquer them, for he is Lord of lords and King of kings, and those with him are called and chosen and faithful.
Revelation 17:14, ESV

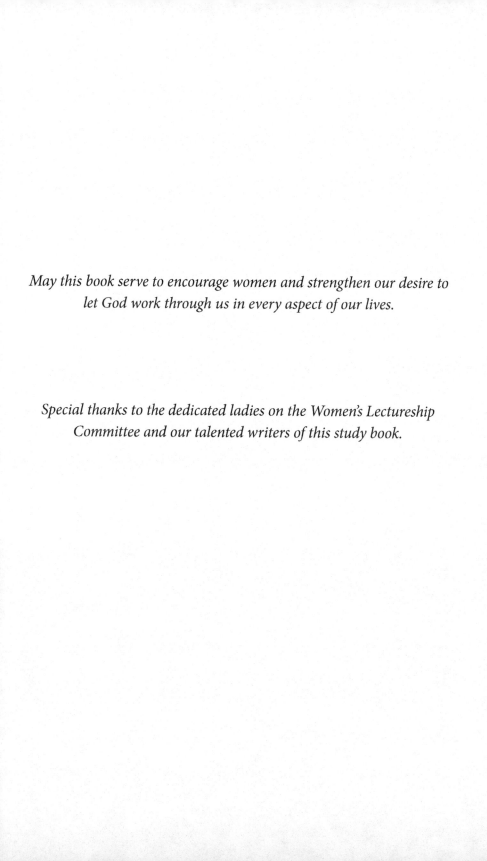

May this book serve to encourage women and strengthen our desire to let God work through us in every aspect of our lives.

Special thanks to the dedicated ladies on the Women's Lectureship Committee and our talented writers of this study book.

88TH ANNUAL

FREED-HARDEMAN
BIBLE LECTURESHIP

February 4-8, 2024

David R. Shannon
President of Freed-Hardeman University

Dr. Doug Burleson
Director of Lectureship
Editor of Lectureship Books

LADIES LECTURESHIP COMMITTEE

Kristi Burleson

Amanda Ketchum

Cathy D. Powell

Laurel Sewell

Tracie Shannon

Aleshia Sokoloski

Becky Welch

Dwina W. Willis

TABLE OF CONTENTS

Welcome
First Lady Tracie Shannon

Change. Some of us love change in all of its adrenaline-pumping possibilities. Some of us shrink back from the inevitable disruption change will bring. However we may feel about it, change is a big part of life. If you're on campus with us this week for the 88th annual Bible Lectureship, you will have noticed lots of changes. Our new dining hall is under construction. We have a new campus store called The Belfry! Hall-Roland, our oldest women's dormitory, is undergoing a complete renovation. We have a new Jazz Band! So many changes! We pray that despite the newness, you will find that the love and familial ties you have always felt on this campus are the same. We love and appreciate you and intend for that to be a constant year after year – we are family.

The heart of these projects is the desire to create a home that students love continually, to tailor spaces that help them thrive in community, love, learning, and fun. We want our students to look around them and see from the beauty of this place that they matter and are worth the continual pursuit of excellence in every area – they are worth spending the money to make change where it's needed. Budgets and sustainability are critical, but the people are at the heart of what takes place here. We want to be like our Father in this way!

At the heart of Revelation is God and his final victory over Satan that allows him to dwell with the people he loves in an unimaginably beautiful new home.

Revelation 21:2-3 "I saw the Holy City, the new Jerusalem, coming down out of heaven from God, prepared as a bride beautifully dressed for her husband. And I heard a loud voice from the throne saying, "Look! God's dwelling place is now among the people, and he will dwell with them. They will be his people, and God himself will be with them and be their God."

God desires to be with us! Revelation teaches us that despite all change on this earth, God's word and the triumph of the Lamb is confirmed, resolute, and guaranteed.

Revelation 21:5-6a "And the one seated on the throne said: "Look! I am making all things new!" Then he said to me, "Write it down, because these words are reliable and true." He also said to me, "It is done! I am the Alpha and the Omega, the beginning and the end...""

I'm deeply grateful to Doug and Kristi Burleson for their dedication and countless hours of work and leadership that makes the Lectureship possible each year.

I offer a heartfelt thank you to the women who will teach us this year through this study book and the daily women's sessions.

Let's prepare our hearts to study together. The hero we cannot live without; the Lamb is taking the stage... Revelation 22:16-17 "I, Jesus, have sent my angel to testify to you about these things for the churches. I am the root and the descendant of David, the bright and morning star!" And the Spirit and the bride say, Come!" And let the one who hears say: "Come!"

Reading Revelation is like hearing a fight song that draws our attention to the battle that is raging and the hope of victory!

Praise God! The Victory is Won!

With much love,

Tracie

DEDICATION 🏛

FHU Associates

The 2024 Annual Bible Lectureship is dedicated to the selfless group of women, past and present, known as the Freed-Hardeman University Associates.

On September 5, 1963, ladies whose husbands were members of the Freed-Hardeman College Board of Trustees and Advisory Board met for the purpose of planning a women's organization to help support and encourage Christian education at Freed-Hardeman College in Henderson, Tennessee. Mrs. Neal Penny of Milan, Tennessee presided at the meeting and was elected the first president. In  late 1963 and early 1964, chapters of the Freed-Hardeman Associates were organized in west Tennessee and Kentucky, and north Alabama and Mississippi. Over the last 60 years the FHU Associates has been made up of career women, stay-at-home moms, retirees, young alumni, and other outstanding women who have put others before themselves.

In his 2020 book titled *By the Grace of God: The Story of Freed-Hardeman University*, Dr. Greg Massey shared that the Associates in its first few years raised funds for a new bus that transported the FHC Chorus, a speech lab, a campus radio station, and funds to build new buildings including Loyd Auditorium and the FHU Associates Science Center (215-16). Since its beginning, the Associates have raised almost $4.5M for student scholarships, while also being a constant source of help for the FHU Lectureship. Whether through their F. H. Brew coffee, the Lectureship kitchen, rummage sales, tea parties, cookbooks, hospitality at the Hardeman House, ladies' Bible study books, Sunshine Boxes, or many other thoughtful means of outreach, the FHU Associates have been a blessing to many. The FHU Associates believe in the power of a Christian education at FHU and have given their time, talents, and financial resources to that end.

Past presidents of National Associates include Margaret Penny, Rebecca Woods, Pearl Griffin, Louise Dixon, Hazel Bradfield, Sylvia Harris, Irene Taylor, Lynda Ruff, Delphia Thornton, Martha Alls, Rubye Dodd, Corine Taylor, Fran Davis, Jo Martin, Lora Edwards, Laurel Sewell, Genia Southall, Ann Watson, Diane Smith, Lana Pirtle, Debbie McLaughlin, Sylvia Scott, Jeanita Estes, Carole Childers, and Shirley Eaton.

Drive to **25**

FHU ASSOCIATES

Spread joy. Encourage friendships.
Support student scholarships.

You can become part of the
FHU Associates' Drive to 25
mission by initiating or joining
a chapter, no matter your
geographical location.

Connect with us at
fhu.edu/associates!

Associates
of FREED-HARDEMAN UNIVERSITY

SERVICE | SUPPORT | FRIENDSHIP *since* 1963

Because He Is Risen, I Will Rise

Revelation 1:17-19

Renee Croom

"When I saw him, I fell at his feet as though dead. But he laid his right hand on me, saying, Fear not, I am the first and the last, and the living one. I died, and behold I am alive for evermore, and I have the keys of Death and Hades. Write therefore the things that you have seen, those that are and those that are to take place "(Rev. 1:17-19). [All scripture references are from the English Standard Version unless otherwise noted.]

HONOR AND THANKS

First, to you, omniscient, omnipresent, and omnipotent God, I give honor and praise. Thank you for giving us the book of Revelation and all its many valuable and applicable lessons. Thank you for being the great God you are, our Savior and Redeemer. In Chapter 1, verses 17-19, you show us that you, eternal

God, possess the power over everything, and because you, all mighty God, have risen, we too shall rise.

Secondly, I must say to you, my dear sisters, it is an honor to have you as fellow heirs of the kingdom of our Lord and Savior, Jesus Christ. Thank you for protecting our heavenly inheritance, salvation. Let us "press on toward the goal for the prize of the upward call in Christ Jesus" (Phil. 3:14).

Sisters, have you ever thought about what life would be like if Jesus had not risen from the dead? Would we be lost eternally? Would our sins be forgiven, or would death become our end? Amazingly, there is no need for us to wonder. Our Savior is risen! The scriptures echo this truth. Christ rose from the dead, "never to die again" (Rom. 6:9). We too shall rise, never to die!

THE MAIN CONFLICT

Death is an enemy to God. He never intended for us to die. Adam and Eve were given direct instructions on how to avoid it and were well versed on its consequences. The conversation Eve had with the serpent, when he asked if God said she could not eat from all the trees in the garden, exemplifies this. She immediately responded by telling him that of the tree of good and evil she was forbidden to eat (Gen. 3:2-3). Satan knew exactly what to do to get Eve to thinking, to doubting. He carefully strategized his tactic by asking a question. If you want to get someone to thinking, just ask a question. And we know the rest of the story in the book of Genesis; she and

Adam ate of the forbidden fruit, bringing the curse of death to mankind. This conflict set off a chain reaction, resulting in the events that take place in Revelation.

HISTORY

It appears that the book of Revelation was written by John, the apostle, while on the island of Patmos. Patmos was located off the Coast of Asia, which is now modern-day Turkey. Some scholars seem to believe that he wrote it while in exile. It was written to the seven churches of Asia Minor, in Ephesus, Smyrna, Pergamon, Thyatira, Sardis, Philadelphia, and Laodicea, who were experiencing extreme and detrimental persecution.

THE VISION

In the first chapter of Revelation, John sees a vision of an angel, who looks like Jesus, the son of man, and he sees seven stars and seven candlesticks. He hears the voice of Jesus, instructing him to send letters to the churches, letters of encouragement, yet letters of chastisement, pointing out the sins of the early Christians. "For the Lord disciplines the one he loves and chastises every son whom he receives" (Heb. 12: 6). The main purpose of the letters was for Jesus to encourage the saints to remain in the faith by reminding them of the heavenly, eternal home that awaits them in glory with him. And, although Jesus instructs John to write specifically to the seven churches, messages found in the letters, are applicable to all Christians, throughout the span of time.

The description John paints of the vision of the angel of Jesus is amazing and mysterious. "He was clothed with a long robe and a golden sash around his chest" (Rev. 1:13). Next, John tells us that "the hairs of his head were white like wool, like snow. His eyes were like a flame of fire. His feet were like burnished bronze, refined in a furnace, and his voice was like the roar of many waters" (Rev. 1:14-15). This great and perplexing vision provides the setting for our verses of emphasis, Revelation 1:17-19. From our study together, it is my prayer that we will see what God wants us to see, and that we will find lessons that will direct and prepare us for our heavenly home.

REVERENCE, COMFORT, AND ETERNAL GOD

"When I saw him, I fell at his feet as though dead. But he laid his right hand on me, saying, fear not, I am the first and the last" (Rev. 1:17).

After John sees the vision of the angel, he responds by falling as if he were dead, giving glory and honor to our Lord, who is worthy. Here, John shows that our God is to be revered and worshipped. "For from him and through him and to him are all things. To him be glory forever. Amen" (Rom. 11:36). "He is great and does wonderful things; he alone is God (Ps. 86:10). Praise him, my sisters, let us praise him for being our great and mighty God. After

John falls, we see that our God is a God of comfort, as Jesus does a beautiful and heartwarming thing, he lays his right hand on John and says, "fear not, I am the first and the last" (Rev. 1:17). You see our God is never too high that he cannot feel our anxiety. "Who is like the Lord our God, who is seated on high, who looks far down on the heavens and the earth?" (Ps. 113: 5-6). "Blessed be the God and Father of our Lord Jesus Christ, the Father of mercies and God of all comfort, who comforts us in all our affliction, so that we may be able to comfort those who are in any affliction, with the comfort with which we ourselves are comforted by God" (2 Cor. 1:3-4). Finally, at the end of our verse of focus, Jesus says that he is the "first and the last," (Rev. 1:17) meaning nothing existed before him. He created all things. He was with the Father in the beginning and of his existence and reign, there is no end. "In the beginning was the Word, and the Word was with God, and the Word was God. All things were made through him, and without him was not anything made that was made" (John 1:1-2).

LOVE, ETERNITY, AND ENCOURAGEMENT

"And the living one. I died, and behold I am alive forever more, and I have the keys of Death and Hades" (Rev. 1:18).

The next verse of emphasis, Revelation 1:18, is the heart of the chapter, because without the events that take place here, mankind would be lost, forever. Here Jesus tells John, "I am he that liveth," (King James Version) meaning he shall never die again, and then, he goes on to say, "and was dead," relating to the crucifixion. I wonder if this took John back in time, the time when he stood with Mary, the mother of Jesus, as they witnessed that horrible and agonizing death that our Lord and Savior suffered for us. I wonder if John thought back to that moment when Jesus commanded him to take care of Mary (John 19:27). I know the death of Jesus makes me think. It makes me think of the love of Jesus, how God the creator, suffered for the creation, dying a death so gruesome that to think of it makes me cringe and cry, yet it makes me think of the greatest example of love that ever existed. As we further examine verse 18 of Revelation, we hear the wonderful words of Jesus, "and behold I am alive forever more" (Rev. 1:18). Do you know the magnitude of this statement and what it means? It validates who Jesus is, our Lord, our Savior, our Redeemer, and the Sealer of our destiny. It confirms for us that because he is risen, we will rise. This verse ends with Jesus letting us know that he is in complete control of everything, even death. He took back the power of death from the devil, who once controlled it because mankind sinned. It was given to him, and may I emphasize the words, given to him. For it was because of sin that he obtained it, but glory be to our Lord and Savior Jesus Christ, who now and forever has "the keys of Death and Hades" (Rev. 1:18). This verse encompasses some of the most important events of the life of Christ, while he was on earth. We see the rising action, he died; the climax, he rose; and the falling action, he is alive forever more, all results of the main conflict that take place in Genesis 3. From these events, I hear Jesus encouraging us. It is almost like I hear him saying, "Hang in there, my children, children that I love. I know you are faced with many trials and tribulations, and some of you will die for me; but rest assuredly, everything is going to be all right. Death is not your end. I made sure of this when I died on the cross for you. You were once lost and banned from heaven, due to sin, but through my death, I bought you back with the price of my blood, releasing you from the curse. It was the only way I could save you. The sacrificial lamb had to be one without sin, without spot, or blemish (1 Pet. 1:19) so only I could save you. By my death and resurrection, I conquered death and the grave, giving me the power over both. Be encouraged my children when you are persecuted; do not give up the fight, even if it means death. Remember, death is not eternal; it is only temporary. I have risen, and so you, likewise, shall rise. I never meant for you to die in the first place, to feel death's horrible pain. Be encouraged my children; a brighter day is coming."

THE VISION, THE LETTERS, AND THE PUNISHMENT

"Write therefore the things you have seen, those that are and those that are to take place after this" (Revelation 1:19).

Then, in the last verse of which we will examine, Jesus commands John to write about the things he saw, "those that are and those to take place" (Rev. 1:19). The things he saw refer to the vision of Jesus, the vision of the seven stars, which represents the angels of the seven churches, and the vision of the seven candlesticks, which represents the seven churches. "The things that are" refers to the seven letters Jesus told John to write to the seven churches. To the church of Ephesus, the letter stated that the church had left its first love, and to the church in Smyrna, the sin of blasphemy was being practiced. To the church in Pergamos and the church in Thyatira, eating things sacrificed to idols, and fornication had been observed by God. The letter to the church in Sardis was about a dead, church, and the letter to the church in Laodicea pointed out members who were lukewarm Christians. However, the church in Philadelphia did not receive a letter of rebuke because they had kept the word of the Lord (Rev. 2-4). As I think about the letters that Jesus wrote, I cannot help but wonder, if God were to write me a personal letter, what would it say? I believe he might say, "Yet I hold this against you (Rev. 2:14). You do not study the word like I told you to do. "Do your best to present yourself to God as one approved, a worker who has no need to be ashamed, rightly handling the word of truth" (2 Tim. 2:15). Next, he might say, and there are times when you say things that you should not. "Let your speech always be gracious, seasoned with salt, so that you may know how you ought to answer each person" (Col. 4:6). "Let no corrupting talk come out of your mouths, but only such as is good for building up, as fits the occasion, that it may give grace to those who hear" (Eph. 4:29). But, after that, I think he would say, "Those whom I love, I reprove and discipline, so be zealous and repent" (Rev. 3:19). And finally, at the end of Revelation 1:19, when Jesus tells John to write about what will take place, this refers to the crown of life we will receive for being obedient and remaining faithful to the end. It also shows us that "the devil who had deceived them will be thrown into the lake of fire and sulfur where the beast and the false prophet are, and they will be tormented day and night forever and ever" (Rev. 20: 10).

From these scriptures of emphasis, Revelation 1:17-19, God gives us so much food for thought and ammunition to walk godly before him. He also gives us a glorious story of triumph, a heart-warming message of God and man reconciling, and a beautiful story of love. At first glimpse, its language is somewhat puzzling, because of the sophisticated symbolism and unique imagery. However, with careful examination and studying, its messages are unmistakable, providing for us valuable and applicable lessons that are significant and crucial for our walk with God on our journey to eternal life. There are many lessons that we can gain from these three verses. Let us examine a few:

THE LESSONS

1. Studying God's word, takes us to a new level. For example, the book of Revelation appears to be confusing, but the more one studies it, the more knowledgeable he or she becomes. When knowledge is acquired, the word can be defended.

2. When we know what God expects, we can fashion our lives, accordingly. In the letters God wrote to the churches, he told them exactly what they needed to do in order to receive eternal

life. We, too, must listen to what God tells us so that we can live with him, eternally, in heaven. The more we are in the word, the more our inheritance is protected.

3. We must honor and revere God. When John saw him, he fell to the ground. Our eternal creator, too awesome for us to comprehend, is worthy of our praise.

4. God knows when we are afraid, and he comforts us, like he did for John, the Apostle.

5. We are going to suffer for the cause of Christ, but we must persevere. The early Christians experienced severe persecution, some to the point of death, but for those who endured, a crown of life awaits them, just like it does for you and me. On a side note, in some parts of the world, Christians are still experiencing high levels of abuse. They are still dying because of their faith.

6. We do not need to fear death: because Jesus is risen, giving him the power over death and Hades.

7. Jesus died and is alive forevermore. This authenticates who he is; we too, must be authenticated by our actions.

8. Jesus proved his great love for us by dying. We must prove our love for him by dying to sin.

9. Jesus suffered; we must suffer too.

10. Our Jesus is risen, and we too shall rise if we do the will of God and hold out until the end.

11. Jesus died because he loves us; we must show others that we love them.

12. Jesus sacrificed his life for us; we must sacrifice our life for him.

13. We are going to live eternally with Jesus.

14. God encouraged the churches in Asia Minor. Likewise, we need to encourage each other.

15. Through obedience, Jesus rose, and by it, we too shall rise.

CONCLUSION

The conclusion of the matter is this, we sinned. Sin brought death into the world. Death caused us to be separated from God, but because of God's love for us, he devised a plan to reconcile us back to him, so he sent his son Jesus, a sacrificial lamb, to die and take away our sins with his blood, the sins of the world, so that we can be saved from death and live eternally with him in heaven. It was the only way it could be done. Jesus died, rose, and destroyed death, redeeming us forever. He did his part, but redemption is, also, dependent on us. We, too, have our part to uphold in this beautiful story of love, the story of Jesus and man, the story that shows that because he is risen, we too shall rise.

QUESTIONS

1. Many Christians around the world are being badly mistreated. Do you pray for those who are being persecuted?

2. John fell to his feet, showing reverence to God. How do you show reverence to our Lord?

3. We learn so much from studying the Bible. Do you or have you thought about studying the Bible with others?

4. The early church suffered persecution. How can we, as Christians, handle persecution?

5. Jesus is a comforter. Do you find yourself comforting others?

6. The good news about Jesus is seen in the book of Revelation. How often do you share this good news with others?

7. Jesus sent letters to the early Christians warning them of their wrongdoings. If he were to send a letter to you, what would it say?

8. We are so blessed to live in America, where we do not suffer as severely as others do in different parts of the world. However, we are persecuted. What are some ways that we suffer persecution in America?

BIBLIOGRAPHY

Hamilton, Jeffrey. *The Revelation Given to John* 2003, 2016. <https://lavistachurchofchrist.org/LVstudies/Revelation/Revelation.htm>.

Hunt, Richard. *Open Doors 2023 World Watch List: What Persecution Christians Face.* 2023. <https://www.google.com/search?q=open+doors+christian+persecution&rlz=1C1GCEB_enUS916US916&oq=o&gs_lcrp=EgZja>.

Smith, Alan. *Letters To The Seven Churches (Revelation Part 1).* 15 Aug. 2021. <://https://www.cruciformcoc.com/sermons/letters-to-the-seven-churches-revelation-part-1>.

Trunnel, Jamie. *25 Bible Verses About Giving God Glory.* 2015. 17 Feb. 2023. <https://ascripturedlife.com/2023/02/17/25-bible-verses-about-giving-god-glory/>.

Renee Croom is the daughter of Cecelia Harris. She and her husband, Marvin have two children, Raven (Cole) and Chantler (Kelcy) and a granddaughter, Chloe. She is an educator in the public school system. Her claim to fame is that she has been a Christian for over fifty years.

Because He Is Living In the Church, How Should I Reflect Him?

Revelation 2-3

Emily Hatfield

"He who has an ear, let him hear what the Spirit says to the churches."
[All Scripture references are from the English Standard Version unless otherwise noted.]

A s many of us as have put on the Lord Jesus Christ in baptism have been added to the Lord's church (Acts 2:41, 47). Thus, when the Spirit instructs the seven churches of Asia in Revelation 2-3, each of us should listen and heed the words. This would have also been true for the Christians in the first century who were members of congregations who received this letter. While individual congregations were specifically addressed, each member of each congregation was responsible for reading and heeding all of the words, not simply the words written to their congregation.

For this reason, these words are as true and powerful for us today as they were for the first Christians who ever read them. As we study through the two chapters mentioned above, we will see just how applicable the words of Jesus are for us today. We will do that by looking at the attributes of Jesus that are shown in seven pictures of the Christ, by examining the ways that each of the congregations either were or were not reflecting Christ in their behaviors, and finally in the promises from Christ that will encourage and empower us in our walk with him.

THE PICTURES OF CHRIST

The One Who Holds the Stars and Walks Among the Lampstands

In Revelation 2:1, Jesus describes himself as the one "who holds the seven stars in his right hand, who walks among the seven golden lampstands." One verse prior, in Revelation 1:20, we are told that the seven stars are the angels of the churches and the lampstands are the churches themselves. It is very encouraging that the Lord would choose to describe himself from the outset as the one who has placed himself among his people. He "walks among" (Rev. 2:1) the congregations, noting their works and loving them deeply. Not simply seeing them, but noticing them and each of their unique works and struggles.

What it means for his people today

As children of the king, we must never forget that the Lord is concerned for his people and mindful of their works and struggles. Not
simply *their* works, though; *your* works. He is the God who holds
and who walks, not the God who *held* and who *walked*. Jesus sees
you, right now, doing the works that you do for and with your congregation. Jesus sees you struggling. Jesus sees you thriving. Wherever you find yourself right now, Jesus sees. Jesus cares. And Jesus
expects that you will be bearing fruit (Luke 13:9).

The First and the Last, Who Died and Came to Life

In Smyrna, many of the Christians were deeply troubled from
without and within; be it from poverty or slanderers or false teachers. To these people, Jesus affirms his deity. He assures them that he
is the firstfruits of those who have fallen asleep (1 Cor. 15:20) and
he will be with them until the moment that they follow him by their
own death and resurrection (Rev. 2:10).

What it means for his people today

There are not many more comforting passages than Revelation
2:10: "Be faithful unto death, and I will give you the crown of life."
Even if the tribulation leads to your death, if you remain faithful
you will receive the crown of life. You can trust the promise of the
one who has died and come back to life never to die again. He is the
one that we can put all of our hope and trust in; the only one! Many

have died; a few have even been raised. But only one has died and risen to die no more! That is our Lord; the very Lord promising victory to those who follow Him.

Him Who Has the Sharp Two-edged Sword

It is never good when Jesus has to come first asserting his authority. It is reminiscent of his actions when he would approach the Pharisees or those who were making his father's house a den of thieves (Matt. 21:13). The church in Pergamum was in need of repentance. Instead of turning a blind eye or accepting them in their sin, Jesus reminds them that his word is authoritative. In Revelation 2:16, he says, "Therefore repent. If not, I will come to you soon and war against them with the sword of my mouth." While most people want the Jesus who is quick to embrace and welcome, or who will hold them when they are hurting, many reject the Jesus who cannot be approached due to the iniquity of the approacher. Jesus reminds all who will listen that his words are to be adhered to. After all, his words are life and truth (John 6:63).

What it means for his people today

Hours before his death on the cross, Jesus prayed to the Father and said, "your word is truth" (John 17:17). All scripture has been breathed out by God for our benefit (2 Tim. 3:16). If we merely study the texts with which we are already familiar, or cling only to the palatable teachings like grace and mercy, we will miss the full helping of God's bountiful message. We will miss his holiness if we never study sin's effects. We will miss his salvation if we never appreciate the lost state in which we once lived. The sum of God's word is truth (Ps. 119:160). We need to extract every ounce of goodness if we will satisfy our souls.

The Son of God, With Eyes like a Flame of Fire and Feet of Burnished Bronze

In Revelation 1:14-15, John describes the appearance of the one speaking to him in his vision. Two of the descriptions are repeated for the church at Thyatira. This congregation, struggling with false teachers and idolatry, needed reassurance that their God could see all things and overpower all things. The penetrating, flaming eyes could see past the seduction of Jezebel and straight to the heart and mind of each individual (Rev. 2:23). The very Son of God was in control, even when other forces seemed strong.

What it means for his people today

There are many forces that seem strong in our world. Worldliness and materialism seduce us time and again. Fornication, greed, bitter envy, jealousy; all of the tools and tactics Satan has used from the beginning he continues to use in congregations today. Be assured, though, that the Son of God has eyes that can see straight to the heart and mind of each person. He knows our struggles and strengthens us in our weaknesses. All authority has been given to him (Matt. 28:18); the authority to save us from our sins and conquer the one who has tried to place his grip on us. Jesus stripped Satan of the only power he ever had — the power of death! Rest in the assurance of God's Son as *your* Savior! Lean into his power instead of trusting in your own.

The One Who Has the Seven Spirits of God and the Seven Stars

Sardis is a congregation that is dead. It is no wonder, then, that Jesus chooses to announce himself as the one who has the perfect and complete Spirit. Throughout the book of Revelation, the number seven often means complete or perfect. In this context, it seems to be referring to the complete nature of the Spirit who is also seeing all that is going on in this congregation. The Godhead sees all that is happening; even when the people might have fooled one another, they could not fool God.

What it means for his people today

There are many within our congregations who have a name that they are alive, but what would Jesus say about them? Knowing that our Lord sees all, and that the Spirit himself also takes note of all that is going on within a person's very thoughts and intents, should make Christians examine themselves to make sure they are in the faith (2 Cor. 13:5). While we can walk into the building on Sunday morning and sit in our sacred spot, we would do well to be sure that the one who sees in tandem with the Spirit is pleased with our actions. Instead of sleepily meandering through life on earth, we must wake up (Rev. 3:2) and get to work.

The Holy One, the True One, Who Has the Key of David

The Psalms are replete with passages about God as the Holy One of Israel (71:22, 78:41, 89:18). Jesus is just as much deity as God the Father and God the Spirit. Not only are his words true, but *he* is true. He is true and he is holy — separate. One thing that makes him set apart is that he has keys that no one else has. Revelation 1:18 states that Jesus has "the keys of Death and Hades." These keys, given to the Son of David, were given as he defeated Satan at his own game, delivering the final crushing blow while Satan merely bruised his heel (Gen. 2:15). The Christians in Philadelphia needed to be reminded that death had no grip on them! The doors Jesus shut would remain shut and the ones he opened would remain so. No one and no thing had power above that of the Holy God. The congregation here could rest in the fact that their Savior was Sovereign!

What it means for his people today

Today, people are prone to try to get in our heads. Naysayers are equipped with tools from the evil one. Satan loves using discouragement as a weapon to weaken the faith of God's elect. We would do well to remember that our God is the holy one, the true one, who has all authority and all power. We need not be discouraged. The one with the keys sets before us open doors, too (Rev. 3:8).

What he opens, we will be able to walk through! Where he sends, he will strengthen. Where he expects us to go, he will equip us to go!

The Amen, the Faithful and True Witness, the Beginning of God's Creation

Jesus is the beginning and the end. He is the Word that was in the beginning with God (John 1:1-2). He is faithful to his promises and the final say on any matter. The Christians in Laodicea were making Jesus sick! He loved them (Rev. 3:19), and because he did, they needed to know that their behavior was unacceptable. Priding themselves on their own prosperity, Jesus reminded them that anything they had was through him, not themselves. Instead of boasting in their material wealth, they should have seen the poverty of their spiritual state. As the Judge, he was giving them a glimpse into what the final verdict would be should they stay on that course.

What it means for his people today

Instead of seeking wealth and prosperity, Christians are to be people seeking Jesus with their whole hearts. Any blessing that is afforded to us in our physical pursuits is just that, a blessing. Lives that belong to Jesus should be lived zealously, giving him everything we have and allowing him to be the one who is our clothing, our salve, and our treasure (Rev. 3:18). Filling ourselves with anything other than Jesus will leave us empty, thinking we are clothed luxuriously, but instead naked and destitute.

A REFLECTION OF CHRIST

The church is described as the bride of Christ (Eph. 5:22-32). In Revelation 2-3, Jesus is pictured as walking among and watching over his bride. He died for her and expects that she will live for him. Is this a true picture of us today? Because Jesus is living in the church, how *should* I reflect him?

A reflection shows only what is in the original image. It is imperative, then, that our lives reflect only what the original image of Jesus shows. From our text, we have seen that Jesus is, among other things, holy, faithful, present, and powerful. Our lives ought to be these things too.

We should be holy; instead of being conformed to the world, we ought to be transformed by the renewing of our minds (Rom. 12:1-2). We are to be faithful to Christ, even if it means death (Rev. 2:10). We trust in his power to save, and thus surrender our lives into his care. As Christ is present, watching and walking among the congregations, we too should be present. We are to be active participants in worship and congregational life, not mere observers or lukewarm lurkers. Finally, we should be powerful. Sure, we cannot be all-powerful like Jesus, but we can exercise the power within us! Paul reminds a timid Timothy in 2 Timothy 1:7, "God gave us a spirit not of fear, but of power and love and self-control." Earlier, Paul wrote to the Romans that they "did not receive the spirit of slavery to fall back into fear, but you have received the Spirit of adoption as sons, by whom we cry 'Abba! Father!'" (Rom.

8:15). Christ wants us to show his power through our unafraid, zealous, bold lives!

THE PROMISES OF CHRIST

Anyone who has an ear, listen to the words that have been directed to the churches! These promises are eternal. Coming from the Amen, the first and last, the Son of God, the faithful and true witness — these promises are rock solid. We can find strength, comfort, and a hunger for God's words as we read these promises that were first given to the churches in Asia, but are sure and true for the church today, too.

These promises are given to the ones who overcome; the ones who are victors in the name of Jesus. Those who come away victorious at the end, who keep his banner held high throughout all of life's battle, these promises are for those Christians. These very promises are meant to keep *you* fighting so that you can be among that number one great and glorious day.

I Will Grant to Eat of the Tree of Life, Which is in the Paradise of God

The tree of life was the sustaining life giver in the garden. Adam and Eve, once tainted by sin, had to leave the garden and the life-giving tree. Sin has always robbed us in this life, but one day that will be over. One day, we will forever eat of the tree of life. Those who conquer will forever be sustained by and in the presence of God. He who has an ear, let him hear!

I Will Not Be Hurt by the Second Death

Death hurts those left behind. Physical separation from loved ones is a deep and abiding grief. In the first century, the deaths that many Christians were subjected to by the hands of torturous Romans were physically hurtful. These were not peaceful transitions, but rather devastatingly splintering: being sawn in two, whipped with glass and sharp rocks, mauled by wild beasts, tortured, or executed by the sword. This promise of Christ was poignant for the Christians of the first century, because excruciating moments could always be lurking days or weeks in their future, but the second death? It could not touch them! The same is true for Christians today. Stand with Christ. Even if it means death, stand with Christ. Only one death will hurt you if you are standing with him. What a glorious and grace-filled promise!

I Will Never Blot His Name Out of the Book of Life

Have you ever felt unworthy? As a sinner, it is likely a regular occurrence to feel overwhelmed by the great love and mercy that our God shows to us. As followers of Christ, we have a promise that Jesus will never blot our names out of the book of life. Sure, we can choose to walk away from him and crucify him again by our actions (Heb. 6:6:). That choice is left up to us. The promise, though, is that Jesus will not walk away. Jesus will not turn his back. Jesus has done the work of saving and shedding his blood to blot out all of our sins, and that is the only blotting he intends to do. His blood was meant to cleanse you of sins, not write you out of the will. Because of this great promise, let us live lives that reflect his goodness and glory; spreading this good news to anyone and everyone who will have an ear to hear!

To the one who conquers, I will make him a pillar in the temple of my God

Psalm 84:10 says, "For a day in your courts is better than a thousand elsewhere. I would rather be a doorkeeper in the house of my God than dwell in the tents of wickedness." God, in his infinite grace and goodness, has allowed us to bypass being doorkeepers and instead invites us as his children to be pillars in the temple; ever abiding in the presence of God. Imagine for a moment that you are living forever in the very presence of God. It is almost unfathomable for the human mind! Yet, Jesus promises those who continue in his service, who remain faithful to the end, that this is their destiny. One day, we get to be forever in heaven with God! Lord, come quickly!

I Will Grant Him To Sit With Me on My Throne

Talk about unworthy! Not only are we promised fruit from the tree of life, and eternal life in the presence of God, but now Jesus says that those who overcome the darkness of this world will be granted this beautiful, intimate access to him. Picture a child, climbing up into the chair with their father. Snuggling in, feeling that place of safety, honor, and privilege as a child. This is the promise given to us. If you belong to Christ, you are a child of God. The Father wants you to be with him forever, basking in his light—the light you have been reflecting your entire walk in Christ.

CONCLUSION

Jesus Christ is walking among his people, concerned with their faithfulness and their trials. He is invested in the life of his bride, desiring desperately that she will remain faithful to him. Through the letters to the seven churches of Asia, we see Jesus showing himself to his people; correcting them when necessary, encouraging them when possible, and promising them life forevermore. What makes the church today any different from the churches we read of in these letters? Only time separates us. The evil one still desires that we follow him. He is using recycled schemes to trip us up and lure us to his side so that we can share in his suffering —a place of weeping and gnashing of teeth that was made for him, not us (Matt. 25:41). Our Lord has a different place prepared for his people.

> Let not your hearts be troubled. Believe in God; believe also in me. In my Father's house are many rooms. If it were not so, would I have told you that I go to prepare a place for you? And if I go to prepare a place for you, I will come again

and will take you to myself, that where I am you may be also. And you know the way to where I am going.

(John 14:1-4)

The promises of Jesus are as true for us today as they were for the Christians reading the words to the seven churches of Asia. Jesus' promises remain true, his descriptions about himself are still accurate, and his commission to us, his bride, is the same. We are to reflect him in all that we do. As the one who is walking around in the midst of his people, he knows the works we are doing. He sees the fruit we are bearing. If we are not bearing fruit, we are called to repentance. If we are, then we are called to remain faithful until death. In all things, in all ways, keeping our eyes firmly fixed on the one who invites us to life with him forever. He who has an ear, let him hear!

QUESTIONS

1. Not every congregation was being faithful to the Lord. Why do you think Jesus gave each of them a promise?

2. Does the fact that Jesus is still watching congregations give you comfort or concern for your own congregation? Why?

3. Some of the pictures of Jesus seem frightening at first glance (flaming eyes, two-edged swords). Should we have a sense of fear when it comes to our Lord?

4. Which church do you find that you identify with the most? Which do you desire to be more like?

5. What is one way you can reflect Christ within your congregation this week?

 **Emily Hatfield** graduated from Freed-Hardeman University in 2010 with a degree in journalism. Since graduating, she has used her education to pursue opportunities in photography, videography, and writing. In 2018, she published a women's devotional book titled, *Exposed: The World's Lies and Deceptions Uncovered.*

Emily and her husband, Robert, married in 2011 and have two children. He is the pulpit minister for the Henderson church of Christ and she is a devoted supporter of his work in the kingdom. In 2013, they co-founded The Light Network, a network of podcasts dedicated to producing Bible-based, culturally relevant content for God's glory. Emily hosts a weekly podcast for women called *Wifey Wednesdays.*

Because He Is Seated On the Throne, What Is My Place?

Revelation 4

Jania Otey

T he <u>Apocalypse</u> to John is filled with numerous visions, imagery, metaphors, similes, and allusions. The figures are prevalent from the beginning of Revelation to the end. The events recorded by John, as revealed by Jesus, are reminiscent of Daniel, Ezekiel, and Zechariah's prophecies. In chapter 4, John provides readers with a glimpse of God's glorious throne. A notable feature of this chapter is the role of created beings who are privileged to be in God's presence.

While the apex of the Apocalypse is Christ's triumph over evil, believers can draw inspiration to continue the fight against Satan and remain steadfast in their obedience to God, in part, due to the grand depiction of the reward that awaits the faithful. John's succinct, yet telling, portrayal of God's throne room illustrates the magnificence of God and the humble function of those who are blessed to serve him.

THE CONTEXT

In chapters 2 and 3, John shares the revelation received from Jesus to the seven churches of Asia Minor. He addresses the churches in Ephesus, Smyrna, Pergamos, Thyatira, Sardis, Philadelphia, and Laodicea. John commends the admirable work of the churches, but he also points out where they have fallen short (Rev. 2:2–6; 2:8–11; 2:12–16; 2:18–22; 3:1–5; 3:7–12; 3:14–19). [All scripture references are from the New King James Version unless otherwise noted]. At the conclusion of chapter 3, Jesus reminds the churches of the privilege and the reward that awaits the faithful in Christ. He writes explicitly, "To him who overcomes I will grant to sit with Me on My throne, as I also overcame and sat down with My Father on His throne" (Rev. 3:21). This is the context of the next chapter. In chapter 4, John describes what will take place after the enemies of God are destroyed.

THE SUMMONS (REVELATION 4:1A)

The focus of chapter 4 is a description of the throne, the one sitting on the throne, the twenty-four elders, and other beings privileged to fellowship with God and Christ. After Jesus dictates seven letters to John, another vision is disclosed to him. John sees a door standing open in heaven and hears a voice speaking directly to him (Rev.

4:1–2). This is described as the "first voice," alerting readers that additional voices will come. This first voice sounds like a trumpet and summons John to "Come up here" (Rev. 4:1). The sound of the trumpets seemingly provides notice that God will speak (cf. Ex. 19:19–20). The commanding and bold sounds of trumpets will also play before the dead in Christ rise for judgment (1 Cor. 15:52; cf. 1 Thess. 4:16). Just as John was called up to heaven in chapter 4, in chapter 11, two witnesses later hear "a loud voice from heaven saying to them, 'Come up here.' And they ascended to heaven in a cloud'" (Rev. 11:12; 4:1). John's experience is somewhat analogous to the two witnesses, yet there is no mention of him going up to heaven via a cloud.

THE VISION (REVELATION 4:1B)

Rev 2:10

The voice informs John, "I will show you what must take place after this" (Rev. 4:1). The voice likely belongs to Jesus. The word "this" in 4:1 refers to Christ's final victory over evil. Interestingly, an earlier vision, in chapter 1, is introduced with similar language. John writes, "I was in the Spirit on the Lord's day, and I heard behind me a loud voice like a trumpet" (Rev. 1:10; cf. 4:1). In both instances, just before John receives the vision, he describes his state as being "in the Spirit" (Rev. 1:10; 4:2). In this context, "in the Spirit" relates to John being in a state to see the vision revealed to him by God through Christ.

THE THRONE'S LOCATION (REVELATION 4:2)

Chapter 4 is significant because John provides insight into the appearance of God's throne. He sees a throne in heaven and someone seated on the throne (Rev. 4:2). However, whether John is physically situated in heaven or not does not affect the import of his message. There are many references to God's throne being in heaven in the Old Testament and the New Testament. For instance, the Psalmist writes, "The Lord has established His throne in heaven, And His kingdom rules over all" (Ps. 103:19). The prophet Isaiah states, "Thus says the Lord: "Heaven is My throne, And earth is My footstool. Where is the house that you will build Me? And where is the place of My rest?" (Isa. 66:1). Matthew also references God's throne and its station in heaven (Matt. 5:34; cf. 23:22). The voice beckoning John to "Come up here," coupled with his description of "a throne [that] stood in heaven," supports the contention that John is having a spiritual experience (Rev. 4:1–2). The text does not indicate that his physical body is in heaven.

THE ONE SITTING ON THE THRONE (4:3A)

John next uses jasper and sardius to describe the magnificent outward appearance of the one who sits at the throne: "And He who sat there was like a jasper and a sardius stone in appearance" (Rev. 4:3a). Jasper is a precious gemstone that is commonly used for ornamentation and comes in many different colors. Sardius and carnelian stones are sometimes referred to interchangeably. However, sardius is usually reddish-brown in color, whereas carnelian has a siliceous reddish-orange hue.

Gemstones are mentioned throughout the Bible and they have various uses. In Exodus, God commissioned Moses to make priestly garments for Aaron and his sons as part of their preparation to serve in this holy capacity (Exod. 28:1–2). Moses decorates the breastplate of righteousness for Aaron's priestly garments with jasper (Exod. 28:15–20; Exod. 39:9–13). In a later vision, John describes the holy city of Jerusalem as "having the glory of God. Her light was like a most precious stone, like a jasper stone, clear as crystal" (Rev. 21:11). Similarly, the foundations of the wall of Jerusalem are decorated with beautiful jasper and carnelian stones (Rev. 21:18–20). While John does not provide additional details in this chapter regarding the appearance of the being sitting on the throne, the reader is impressed with a sense of God's majesty, beauty, and radiance.

THE SURROUNDINGS (REVELATION 4:3B)

John also describes what appears around the throne: "and there was a rainbow around the throne, in appearance like an emerald" (Rev. 4:3b). He uses another similie and a different gemstone as he observes a rainbow that appears like an emerald. John's vision of the rainbow in Revelation chapter 4 is reminiscent of Genesis chapter 9. After God flooded the earth due to humanity's wickedness, God told Noah, "I set My rainbow in the cloud, and it shall be for the

sign of the covenant between Me and the earth ... and I will remember My covenant which is between Me and you and every living creature of all flesh; the waters shall never again become a flood
to destroy all flesh" (Gen. 9:13–15). In addition to jasper and carnelian, various precious stones, including emeralds and sardius,
line the foundation of Jerusalem's wall (Rev. 21:19–20).

Like jasper, emeralds are expensive stones, but a distin-
guishing feature is the transparency of emeralds. Perhaps the trans-
parent nature and the emerald's hue is why that stone is used in
John's rainbow depiction. The luminous green rainbow in John's
vision is situated around the throne. In the Old Testament, the
prophet Ezekiel uses the beauty of a rainbow and the brilliance of a
sapphire stone to depict the glory of God and the magnificence of
his throne (Ezek. 1:28; 10:1). John's use of precious stones to describe what appears around the throne and in Jerusalem are reminders of God's majesty and the sacred place that awaits Christians who are delivered from evil.

The beautiful emerald rainbow around the throne may also
serve as a reminder of how God always honors his covenants. He
protected Noah and his family from dying in the flood because
Noah found grace in God's eyes, and he was a preacher of righteousness (Gen. 6:5–8; cf. Heb. 11:7; cf. 2 Pet. 2:5). God has kept his
promise never to destroy all flesh with water again. Likewise, John's
depiction of the rainbow around the throne can help Christians reflect on and hold fast to God's promise that he will ultimately deliver
the righteous from evil in the final triumph over Satan and his angels.

THE AUDIENCE AROUND THE THRONE (REVELATION 4:4)

In the next verse, John reveals that twenty-four thrones are situated around the great throne, and twenty-four elders have the honor of occupying the subordinate thrones (Rev. 4:4). John mentions the twenty-four elders several times later in the Apocalypse (Rev. 4:10; 5:8; 5:14; 11:16; 19:4). The color of their robes is noteworthy. John writes, "I saw twenty-four elders sitting, clothed in white robes" (Rev. 4:4). The white garments seem to symbolize the purity of the elders. Their garments are not soiled. The church in Sardis is a stellar example. John writes, at the behest of Jesus, "You have a few names even in Sardis who have not defiled their garments; and they shall walk with Me in white for they are worthy (Rev. 3:4). Similarly, Paul describes how the church will be presented to Christ "not having spot or wrinkle or any such thing, but that she should be holy and without blemish" (Eph. 5:27). John's vision of the audience around the throne is a reminder for believers to walk in the light as God is in the light so that the blood of Jesus can cleanse us of all unrighteousness (cf. 1 John 1:7; cf. Eph. 5:8–9). The continual cleansing by Jesus' blood will afford Christians the honor of being clothed in white and occupying a seat around the throne.

Jesus died to remove the filth of sin from believers, including the twenty-four elders mentioned throughout Revelation. Jesus' blood allows the sinners to be in the presence of God without spot or wrinkle as part of his glorious church—the bride of Christ (cf. Eph. 5:27). Interestingly, although sin, weakness, and vulnerabilities to evil permeate the seven churches of Asia, the Lord is still able to identify Christians worthy to walk with him in white garments (Rev. 3:4; cf. 1 Pet. 4:18). Amid troubles in a world full of wickedness and churches struggling with sin, the righteous still have white garments waiting for them as Jesus triumphs over evil.

In addition to white garments, the twenty-four elders are adorned with golden crowns. The Epistle of James, like Revelation, is filled with figurative language and encourages believers to endure temptation so that they can obtain a crown of life. James writes, "Blessed is the man who endures temptation; for when he has been approved, he will receive the crown of life which the Lord has promised to those who love Him" (Jas 1:12). The author of James writes to exhort and encourage Christians who are scattered outside of Palestine due to persecution (i.e., Acts 8:1–4; Acts 11:19; Jas. 1:1; cf. Psa. 147:2; Isa. 49:6; John 7:35). From the stoning of Stephen to Saul's persecution of the church, Christians were indeed scattered.

The references to trials, sinful behavior permeating the church, and the admonition to stay faithful in spite of their displacement resemble some of the problems in John's vision regarding the seven churches in Revelation. James tells believers that God expects his children never to question his character but to trust in him and maintain one heart—especially in the face of trials and persecution (cf. Jas. 1:5–8). John and James both illustrate that crowns are one of the rewards for suffering and steadfastness—one is golden, and the other is a crown of life. Both crowns seem to symbolize finality on earth and the prize for faithfulness—spending eternity in heaven with the Father (cf. 2 Tim. 4:8; cf. 1 Cor. 9:25;

John 3:16; 1 John 5:11–13; cf. Matt. 7:13–14; cf. Gal. 6:8; cf. Rom. 6:23; cf. 1 John 2:25).

THE SEVEN SPIRITS OF GOD (REVELATION 4:5–7)

After John describes the elders, he observes lighting, hears thunder, and notes voices resounding from the throne: "And from the throne proceeded lightnings, thunderings, and voices" (4:5a). Situated before the throne are also lamps of fire. John writes, "Seven lamps of fire were burning before the throne, which are the seven Spirits of God" (Rev. 4:5b). The number seven is prevalent throughout the Bible and is prominent in Revelation. Specifically, there are thirty-six references to the number "seven" or "seventh" alone (e.g., seven lampstands (Rev. 1:13); seven stars (Rev. 1:16); seven seals (Rev. 5:5); seven angels (Rev. 8:2). Some scholars assert that seven symbolizes completeness or perfection (Morris 48; Mounce 68). In the opening chapter of Revelation, John addresses the seven churches in Asia (Rev. 1:4). His address is specific to select churches. However, Morris contends that the number seven in this context includes a wider audience, not just the seven named in the vision. Morris writes, "[Revelation] is addressed to seven churches in Asia Minor, and while clearly it was meant from the beginning for a wider circle, it is equally clear that it was meant as a serious communication to these churches" (48).

Although the apostle Paul instructs the saints at Ephesus that there is one Spirit (Eph. 4:4), the widely accepted view is that the seven Spirits in Revelation denote the Holy Spirit (Mounce 69). In John's opening salutation to the seven churches in Asia Minor, he greets them on behalf of the godhead, "Him who is and who was and who is to come, and from the seven Spirits who are before His throne" (Rev. 1:4). Similarly, John greets the church at Sardis and announces that the epistle is written at the direction of Jesus who possess the Holy Spirit: "These things says He who has the seven Spirits of God and the seven stars: 'I know your works, that you have a name that you are alive, but you are dead'" (Rev. 3:1). John's letter to each of the seven churches ends by referring to the singular Spirit, "He who has an ear, let him hear what the Spirit says to the churches" (Rev. 2:7; 2:11; 2:17; 2:29; 3:6; 3:13; 3:22). Jesus and the Holy Spirit (in whatever form God deems appropriate) are all present around the throne of God.

In addition to the seven Spirits, John notes: "Before the throne there was a sea of glass, like crystal" (Rev. 4:6a). In a later vision, he sees a sea of glass mixed with fire, along with the victors who prevail against the beast standing next to the glassy sea (Rev. 15:2). Four creatures are positioned in the center of the throne and around the throne. John indicates that the living creatures are "full of eyes in the front and in the back" (Rev. 4:6b). The creatures are distinct, each having their own unique appearance: "The first living creature was like a lion, the second living creature like a calf, the third living creature had a face like a man, and the fourth living creature was like a flying eagle" (Rev. 4:7).

PRAISING GOD AROUND THE THRONE (REVELATION 4:8–11)

The creatures around the throne praise God continually. John writes, "The four living creatures, each having six wings, were full of eyes around and within. And they do not rest day or night, saying: 'Holy, holy, holy, Lord God Almighty, Who was and is and is to come!'" (Rev. 4:8; cf. Rev. 1:4). The word "holy" in Revelation 4:8 denotes "God's incomparable majesty" (Thayer 6). W. E. Vines writes, "It is predicated of God (as the absolute Holy One, in His purity, majesty and glory)" (556). The glory of God fills the entire universe that he created. The word glory denotes God's abundant splendor. The creatures around the throne will have the honor of witnessing God's majesty for eternity.

The living creatures not only praise God continually, but John also notes that they "give glory and honor and thanks to Him who sits on the throne, who lives forever and ever" (Rev. 4:9). Every time the living creatures give glory, honor, and thanks to God, the twenty-four elders previously mentioned participate in displaying their adoration for the Most High. For instance, John writes, "the twenty-four elders fall down before Him who sits on the throne and worship Him who lives forever and ever, and cast their crowns before the throne, saying: 'You are worthy, O Lord, To receive glory and honor and power; For You created all things, And by Your will they exist and were created'" (Rev. 4:10–11).

While in exile in the land of the Chaldeans, the prophet Ezekiel also saw "visions of God" (Ezek. 1:1). In one of his first vision episodes, Ezekiel describes four living creatures with wings, each having four faces in the likeness of a human, a lion, an ox, and an eagle (Ezek. 1:1; 1:5–11). John's revelation about the creatures is distinguishable from Ezekiel's vision, in part, because John observes that the creatures praise God perpetually.

In a similar vision, the prophet Isaiah describes the Lord sitting high on the throne in the temple with seraphim ministering to him (Isa. 6:1–3). One of the seraphim exclaimed to another seraphim, "Holy, holy, holy is the Lord of hosts; The whole earth is full of His glory!" (Isa. 6:3). The living creatures and seraphim (which are a type of angelic being) minister to God and shower him with praise because he is seated on the throne. The throne represents the highest authority and God's undeniable power.

MY FUNCTION AROUND THE THRONE

John's vivid description of the one sitting on the throne should spur a spirit of humility in Christians as they reflect on God's majesty. The grandeur of the throne's surroundings serves as a reminder of God's glory and power. The detailed depictions of the audience around the throne confirm the prophecies in the Old Testament. John's depictions also remind Christians of the privilege that awaits the righteous in heaven after the final triumph of the Lamb. By reading and studying the Apocalypse to John, Christians can seek motivation and inspiration to keep their garments free from the unfruitful works of darkness and to walk circumspectly in their labor and work for the Lord (cf. Eph. 5:11; cf. 1 Cor. 15:58; cf. Eph. 15:15).

John's letter helps believers who eagerly await Christ's final victory over evil envision their place in eternity. Faithful believers will lay prostrate at the feet of God and praise him continually, just as the elders and spiritual beings described by John and the prophets of old. What an honor and privilege the saints in Christ will have to worship God. What an honor and privilege to lay at his feet and shower him with praise and thanksgiving, never ceasing to acknowledge his worth, his power, and that he is the creator of all things.

God affords man ample opportunity to obey and reverence him. He even humbles man to open his eyes to the truth of God's word. God is the "the Alpha and the Omega, the Beginning and the End," says the Lord, 'who is and who was and who is to come, the Almighty'" (Rev. 1:8). Believers who love God and recognize his authority, will relish in the opportunity to occupy their place around the throne to worship, praise, and constantly acknowledge his goodness and might.

CONCLUSION

Chapter 4 of the Apocalypse to John provides readers with a picturesque preview of God's glorious throne and the created beings who serve him. John's vision of God's majesty and the role of the faithful in Christ as prophesied by Daniel, Ezekiel, and Zechariah should reassure believers that God will reward their perseverance through trials. Christians would do well to use John's vision as a reminder never to forget the holiness of God. His vision should also spur Christians to love God wholeheartedly, serve God diligently while on earth, and live in a manner that will allow them to occupy a seat around God's glorious throne.

QUESTIONS

1. Read Revelation 4:1. Explain what "this" refers to, considering the previous chapters in Revelation. Use scriptures to support your answer.

2. How is a Christian's function similar to the living creatures John describes in Rev. 4:8? Should Christians wait until Jesus' final triumph over evil to praise and honor God?

3. What will be the role of Christians who have the privilege to be in the presence of God around his throne? Use at least three scriptures from the Old and New Testaments to support your answer.

4. John provides many details about who and what is around and before the throne. Find and discuss additional visions and prophecies related to the throne in scripture. How can John's descriptions inspire and encourage Christians to stay faithful?

5. What lessons should Christians learn from chapter 4? Include at least three people in scripture to support your answer.

BIBLIOGRAPHY

Morris, Leon. *Revelation: An Introduction and Commentary*. Downers Grove, IL: IVP Academic, 2007.

Mounce, Robert H. *The Book of Revelation*. The New International Commentary on the New Testament 17. Grand Rapids: Eerdmans, 1977.

Thayer, Joseph Henry. *Greek-English Lexicon of the New Testament*. Peabody: Hendrickson, 1999.

Vine, W. E. *Vine's Expository Dictionary of Old & New Testament Words*. Nashville: Thomas Nelson, 1997.

 **Jania Otey** is a native of Clovis, California and lived in Washington, D.C. for 21 years. Jania grew up in the church and obeyed the gospel at an early age. She holds a BA degree in Political Science and a Juris Doctor degree from Howard University. She is admitted to practice law in Maryland and D.C.

Jania has authored a vegan cookbook and published articles in *The Gospel Journal*. Jania and Melvin have two sons, Caleb James and Christian Joseph and they worship with the Perry Hill Road church of Christ. Jania devotes most of her time to educating and shaping the hearts of her sons, being a wife, working in the church, and serving as the Founder and CEO of Kids & Culture, an education enrichment program for children. She lives in Montgomery, Alabama and her biggest accomplishment in life has been introducing the gospel to her husband.

Because He Is Sovereign In Suffering, How Can I Respond To Suffering?

Revelation 7:13-17

Sara Whitworth

P hew. This is a hard topic. I'll be honest: I questioned whether I should accept the invitation to speak and write for the lectureship. This topic is very, very personal to me. Unfortunately, as a friend reminded me recently, I am well acquainted with suffering, especially with grief and loss. They've been constant traveling partners with me for almost a decade now and I haven't always gotten it right. Surely there is someone more qualified than me? But then I reminded myself that our greatest testimony can be sharing our imperfections with others and showing how God has still been able to use us. I am not perfect, I am broken. But with repentance and dedication to the Lord, he has been able and will continue to do good with me. So here I am writing, hoping that what I have to share will be encouraging to you and provide you with hope as you endure suffering in this life.

It can be difficult to know what the appropriate, Christ-like way is to respond to suffering, and even more difficult to make the decision to respond that way. I'm in no way an expert on this subject, but I do want you to know that if you are suffering, you are not alone. I have experienced child loss, betrayal and divorce, miscarriage, and more, so please know that I can empathize with your suffering. I am not naïve to think that this is an easy task or something that we can change quickly. Life can be extremely difficult—just turn on the news and you'll hear about natural disasters, school shootings, war zones, murder, corruption, fraud, and much more almost daily. Read the church bulletin and you will find illness, death, unemployment, and more. Honestly, just sit down with a sister in Christ to share a cup of coffee, and I know she will have some trials that she is currently facing. Suffering is everywhere, it is real and painful, and it can easily overwhelm us if we let it.

When we read the Bible, we see many others who have gone before us who have been through difficult times as well. One of my favorite chapters, Hebrews 11, is filled with examples of faithful followers who suffered but did not give up. In addition, I believe Psalm 88 is a psalm that has been given to us as sufferers to provide us with hope. These chapters show us that what we are going through as Christians and what we are feeling is normal and that we are not alone. "We should all take comfort in the fact that the Bible never treats suffering as anything but a real, significant, and often life-changing human experience." (Tripp). I know that the devil is working hard to break us all, and he knows exactly what trials and tribulations will affect us all the most. Yet we are not the first to experience these types of suffering and we can overcome these struggles with Jesus.

It's hard to imagine sometimes, but the Bible is clear that Jesus suffered so much more than we have (Heb. 2:9). [All Scripture references are from the English Standard Version unless otherwise noted.] Christ took on God's wrath that should have been for us. In Galatians 3:13, we are told that he took on that wrath by suffering on the cross, "Christ redeemed us from the curse of the law by becoming a curse for us – for it is written, 'Cursed is everyone who is hanged on a tree.'" This is truly the greatest possible display of God's glory and grace. He took on our sins and bought our forgiveness by dying the cruelest death possible. He gives us his perfect cloak of righteousness by his suffering. He took away the sting of death by his suffering. He defeated Satan by his suffering. He paid the price for us. Even through all of this unthinkable pain, Christ remained faithful, and his response is the perfect example of how we can respond to our suffering.

So, let's dig into our topic starting with God's sovereignty. What exactly is sovereignty and why does it matter? One of my favorite definitions of sovereignty comes from John Piper on his *Desiring God* website. Piper says that sovereignty means that "God is powerful and authoritative to the extent of being able to override all other powers and authorities." Nothing can stop God or get in his way of accomplishing his will. Isaiah 46:9-10 tells us to "remember the former things of old; for I am God, and there is no other; I am God, and there is none like me, declaring the end from the beginning and from ancient times things not yet done, saying, 'My counsel shall stand, and I will accomplish all my purpose.'" God has had a plan for all of us since before creation. As Christians, we trust that he is in control, has authority of everything and everyone, and he knows best. Romans 8:28 reminds us that "for those who love God all things work together for good, for those who are called according to his purpose." And even farther in the chapter we are told that nothing at all can separate us from God's everlasting love. It's easy to read these verses and say we understand them intellectually (or at least sort of understand them), but when suffering occurs, it can be a challenge to trust God and believe that things will work out (especially if you've been waiting for things to work out for what seems like forever).

Once we are convinced of the reality of God's sovereignty, we then need to ask the question: how should we respond when we suffer? The first word I think of is "preparation." When trials and hardships hit, we must already have a developed faith and trust in God. To prepare for suffering effectively, we must be embedding God's truths in our hearts long before we face the horrible pain. I'll be honest, when my son died, I did not pull out my Bible to do much study for several months. I was just trying to survive, and I believe it is the same with most people. When we are in the thick of things, that is not when we're going to be able to build our foundations and fully grasp biblical truth, but if we dedicate ourselves to study and prayer beforehand, we will know the true biblical theology of suffering and then our hearts and minds will be more prepared when pain or loss come. We might still be surprised or caught off guard, but we will know how to respond, how to trust that Christ will help us through any suffering.

To trust Christ, we must really know him and know his nature. I am convinced of his nature. I am convinced that he is good. I am convinced that he is the same yesterday, today, and forever. I am convinced that he is there with me as I am suffering (even if I cannot feel his presence). I am convinced that he loves me so much that he died for me. And because of these convictions, I can choose to believe that he will work all things together for good even when I can't see the whole picture. As we can see, preparing our faith ahead of time is key to surviving suffering successfully.

The second word I think about when it comes to our response to suffering is "promise." In Revelation 7, we are presented with an inspiring picture: a great multitude of people from all nations, more than we could ever count. These people are all clothed in white robes, holding palm branches in their hands, and crying out saying, "Salvation belongs to our God who sits on the throne, and to the Lamb!" So, who are these people? And what can we learn from them?

In verse 14, we are told that this multitude of people are those who have come out of the great tribulation. Many scholars believe that this scene symbolizes Christians who were martyred, definitely people that we could learn from when we are suffering. When we think about God's promises, we generally think about the blessings that we will be given, such as eternal life or God's grace. Yet, in John 16:33, Jesus promises something different, "I have said these things to you, that in me you may have peace. In the world you will have tribulation. But take heart; I have overcome the world." This is the promise we must believe: We will have tribulation; we are guaranteed suffering. This is not what any of us want to hear, but it is reality, and it does come with a confirmation that Jesus has conquered the world.

A third aspect of suffering is "purpose." If you're like me, you wonder, what is the meaning of all of this suffering? Why can't we just live good lives as Christians and go to heaven? Is that too much to ask? Tim Keller explains that, "Suffering is at the very heart of the Christian faith. It is not only the way Christ became like and redeemed us, but it is one of the main ways we become like him and experience his redemption." (Keller 163). The apostle Paul also reminds us in Philippians 3:10 of the purpose of our suffering, "that I may know him and the power of his resurrection, and may share his sufferings, becoming like him in his death." In Romans 8:17, he says, "and if children, then heirs – heirs of God and fellow heirs with Christ, provided we suffer with him in order that we may also be glorified with him." If we share in suffering with Christ, we also get to share in his glory too!

I absolutely love the example of service that we see in Revelation 7:15. Even after tribulation, this multitude continues to serve

God all day and night. It can be easy to give up and try to distance ourselves from others when we are going through hard times, but here we see that faithful Christians choose to continue to serve God in the midst of their suffering. When we choose to serve, we are taking the focus off ourselves and focusing on others. I'm reminded of Jesus' example of washing the apostles' feet right before he was betrayed. When we chose to serve others during difficult times, this service is a demonstration of our humility and an overflow of our love for God. I also believe that this is how the gospel is fully shown in our lives. We will be showing others that, even in hardship, we will continue to follow Christ's example. By doing so our souls are encouraged. We are not destroyed, we are not crushed, we are not going to give up. We will serve because Jesus served.

A fourth aspect of responding suffering is our "perspective." Returning to the multitude in Revelation 7, in verse 14 we are also told about how their robes have been washed and made white in the blood of the lamb. They have been changed. With suffering we have two options for how we let it change us: (1) I can let this break me/separate me from God, or (2) I can let this refine me/draw me closer to God. It all comes down to the perspective we choose. In Tim Keller's book: *Walking with God through Pain and Suffering*, he offers a different perspective on surviving trials that I found very helpful:

> The Bible calls trials and troubles "walking through fire" or "a fiery ordeal." But it also likens suffering to a fiery furnace. The biblical understanding of a furnace is more what we

would call a "forge". Anything with that degree of heat, is of course, a very dangerous and powerful thing, However, if used properly, it does not destroy. Things put into the furnace properly can be shaped, refined, purified, and even beautified. This is a remarkable view of suffering, that if faced and endured with faith, it can in the end only make us better, stronger, and more filled with greatness and joy. Suffering, then, actually can use evil against itself. It can thwart the destructive purposes of evil and bring light and lift out of darkness and death. (Keller 8)

I loved this perspective from Keller because I am trying hard to let my life experiences shape me into a better person that is more like Christ instead of letting those experiences destroy me. I try to remind myself that when we look at the examples of Joseph in slavery, Daniel in the lion's den, and Shadrach, Meshach, and Abednego in the fiery furnace, these men all went through immense suffering, God did not remove the suffering from their lives, but he did save them in their suffering. The same can be true for us: we might not have the suffering removed from our lives, but God can still save us and mold us as we go through suffering.

It is also important to remember to maintain hope and believe that better times are on their way. We don't know when our suffering will end. It might be next week, it might be in ten years, it might not be until we are united with God in heaven. But we are promised that "the sufferings of this present time are not worth comparing with the glory that is to be revealed to us" (Rom. 8:18).

And God promises that faithful Christians will be comforted from suffering. Isaiah 25:8 also talks about how God will provide comfort to faithful followers, "He will swallow up death forever; and the Lord God will wipe away tears from all faces, and the reproach of his people he will take away from all the earth, for the Lord has spoken." That knowledge has given me so much peace, and I am constantly looking forward to the day when I will see God's glory!

I recently was given a chance to record an album with the Praise & Harmony Singers. Maybe we sounded like the Revelation 7 multitude crying out with loud voices to God? One can hope! Anyway, after divorcing, my daughters and I have moved back in with my parents and I have often felt disconnected and alone by being away from my Christian friends. I thought participating in the vocal group would give me an opportunity to meet other Christians and just have a good time. I also love to sing and have always felt closer to God as I'm singing. When I auditioned for the recording, I had no idea which songs we would be singing, but I just felt that this was something that I should do. We ended up having almost 400 singers that recorded in Texas over Labor Day weekend and we sang 25 songs that were almost all new to me. The most amazing part was that the title of the new album is "Fortress God," and every song is focused on how God is our safe place, how he is who we trust, he will be with us always and guide us, and how he is our refuge and strength. Little did I know that auditioning would turn out to be one of the best decisions I made in 2023. I spent months singing these songs which reinforced God's truth that God is for me; that as a weary traveler I won't be weary long; that death is defeated; that in my weakness God will defend me; that his love surrounds me, and that God will give me joy. "For the Lamb in the midst of the throne will be their shepherd, and he will guide them to springs of living water, and God will wipe away every tear from their eyes." (Rev 7:17). What a comfort and blessing to focus on!

Many times, when we go through suffering, we tend to be inward focused. It's easy to fill our minds with thoughts like: "I can't believe I'm going through this!", "This isn't fair!", "How come _____ has it so easy?", "I wish they knew just how hard I have it!" But I have a positive way to change how you view suffering. We can choose how we react. Even when we cannot control what is going on around us, we can control our emotions. And just like Jesus, when we respond to suffering in faith, our example can be a survival guide for others who are suffering. You might not realize it, but others see how you positively react to suffering, they will notice something different in you, and you will have friends asking you how you have been able to move forward. This is a gift you have been given, and when we recognize that, we can show others a positive way to make it through hard times, to point others to Jesus instead of focusing on our struggles. It will help with your recovery and ultimately show others God's glory. We each go through different life events, and you get to be a unique example to others on how to respond to suffering in a way that honors God. I want to encourage you if you are going through hard times to continue keeping your focus on Christ and look for ways that you can bring glory to him. If you are not suffering at the moment, I want you to look for ways to bring him glory and try to bring comfort to others who are suffering.

We will all go through hard times, but as sisters in Christ, we can work together to build each other up in good times and in bad times! And in order to respond to suffering, remember these words: preparation, promise, purpose, and perspective. "Now may the Lord of peace himself give you peace at all times in every way. The Lord be with you all" (2 Thess. 3:16)!

QUESTIONS

1. Romans 8 tells us that suffering is inevitable. Why do you think that God doesn't remove all suffering?

2. How can you prepare yourself for suffering?

3. How can you use your suffering to help others?

4. What is something you can do to remind you of the purpose of suffering?

5. Each of us can allow suffering to draw us closer to God or drag us away. Which has been true for you? What specific things do you need to change to allow him to draw you closer through your pain?

BIBLIOGRAPHY

Keller, Timothy. *Walking with God through Pain and Suffering*. Penguin, 2013.

Piper, John. "What is the Sovereignty of God?". *Desiring God*. 2019. 8 August 2023. <https://www.desiringgod.org/interviews/what-is-the-sovereignty-of-god>.

Tripp, Paul David. *Suffering*. Wheaton: Crossway, 2018.

Sara Whitworth resides in Bonita Springs, Florida where she works remotely as an Assistant Vice President for Citibank. Sara is the mother of four beautiful children: Daniel, Audrey, Mikaela, and Autumn. Sara served as a minister's wife for 12 years and now attends and serves as a member of the Gulf Coast church of Christ.

Sara has been active in the Lord's church her entire life, and she has a strong passion for ministry, grief/trauma recovery, and mission work. Her mission efforts have taken her as far as Ghana, West Africa, where she was able to use her studies to teach women and children about Christ.

Sara loves the Lord and his people with all of her heart. She is passionate and humbled by opportunities that she receives to share her experiences. She prays that every lesson she presents will bring hope to others and glory to God.

Because He Is Governing The Cosmos, How Do I Live in This World?

Revelation 8:6-9:21

Peggy Tidwell

We've gathered here today to explore one of the most intricate, vibrant, and awe-inspiring sections of the Bible: Revelation 8:6 through 9:21. The topic we are exploring is a thought-provoking and timeless one: "Because He is Governing the Cosmos, How Do I Live in This World?" As women of faith, we constantly seek answers to questions that have echoed through the ages. We live in a world of chaos, but we know that the Almighty God controls the entire cosmos. Join us as we delve into this topic and seek to find ways to navigate this world with confidence and faith in God's sovereignty. We will explore the depths of this age-old question, drawing from biblical truths and personal experiences to find practical guidance for living in a constantly changing world.

SEVEN ANGELS WITH TRUMPETS

Let's dive into the Revelation 8:6-9:21 text. It's quite a surreal sequence of events! In this passage, there are seven angels who each hold a trumpet. With the sound of each trumpet, a new calamity hits the earth. It all begins with the first trumpet that brings "hail and fire mixed with blood" to the earth (Rev. 8:7) [All Scripture references are from the English Standard Version unless otherwise noted.] and ends with the locusts released by the fifth trumpet that torment those without the seal of God (Rev. 9:4). As you read, you'll notice that the text is filled with apocalyptic symbols and events.

APOCALYPTIC SYMBOLS AND EVENTS

The book of Revelation is a complex and often perplexing text that can be difficult to comprehend at first glance. It is easy to overlook it as only symbolic or allegorical and focus instead on more "practical" scriptures. However, let's take the time to understand Revelation's dramatic portrayal of God's sovereignty over the universe. We can gain a deep insight into how we should live our daily lives. This understanding can be precious for women of faith, who often serve as emotional, spiritual, and sometimes literal caregivers in a world that can feel as chaotic as the scenes depicted in Revelation. By studying Revelation, we can better understand God's purposes and how we fit into them, giving us a greater sense of meaning and direction.

Let's consider the opening verse of this sequence: "The first angel blew his trumpet, and there followed hail and fire, mixed with blood, and these were thrown upon the earth" (Rev. 8:7). What an incredible scene this creates. It's important to note that this does not depict a god of wrath arbitrarily throwing down calamities. Instead, this sequence is a vivid reminder of God's control over even the most extraordinary elements. Every hailstone, every flame, every drop of blood is within the scope of God's dominion.

The text continues to describe events such as a great star named Wormwood falling and making the waters bitter, leading to death. "The third angel blew his trumpet, and a great star fell from heaven, blazing like a torch, and it fell on a third of the rivers and on the springs of water" (Rev. 8:10). Even celestial bodies, which have been a source of wonder for mankind throughout history, are under His control. In an era when we worry about environmental pollution and scarcity of natural resources, this serves as a striking image of the consequences of turning away from God and his ultimate authority over the natural world.

Then, there is the trumpet that releases the locusts, an enduring Biblical symbol for a plague that punishes and disrupts. "They were told not to harm the grass of the earth or any green plant or any tree, but only those people who do not have the seal of God on their foreheads" (Rev. 9:4). This plague, terrifying as it may sound, is limited by divine command, reminding us that God's judgments are targeted. He is not a god of indiscriminate destruction but one of purposeful action, and there is comfort to be found in that.

The sounding of the seventh trumpet is a significant event in the Bible. It signals the culmination of everything and serves as a reminder of God's redemptive plan despite the chaos and suffering. The seventh trumpet signifies the reign of God and his Christ and the final judgment. It is a powerful symbol that represents the end of the world as we know it.

Each trumpet that sounds serves as a harbinger of doom and a call to repentance. It reminds us that we need to turn away from our sinful ways and seek forgiveness from God. The sound of the trumpets is a warning that we need to change our ways and live according to God's will.

The seventh trumpet is the most significant because it marks the end of the age. It is the final trumpet that will sound, and it announces the return of Christ. It is a call to all believers to be prepared for his return and to live a life that pleases him. The sound of the seventh trumpet is a reminder that God is in control, and his plan for redemption is still in motion, even amidst the chaos and suffering.

UNDERSTANDING GOD'S SOVEREIGNTY

The intricate and vivid images described in the text, accompanied by the following consequential events, pose a significant question that demands our attention: what is the main message for us, particularly as women in the Lord's church? It is not just about grasping the prophetic or acquiring theological knowledge. Instead, it is about delving deeper into the depth of God's sovereignty as portrayed in these apocalyptic scenes. This understanding empowers us to lead lives of profound faith, integrity, and action. It serves as a reminder that no matter what challenges we face—personal struggles, family problems, or broader societal and global issues—we can trust God's ultimate control and guidance. The detailed and intricate descriptions of the apocalyptic scenes provide us with a glimpse of God's majesty and power, which is something to be admired and contemplated and actively incorporated into our daily lives.

We are called to respond to this divine governance not with passivity but with a renewed commitment to trust him, live righteously, and build a legacy of faith. Whether we are mothers, daughters, sisters, friends, or leaders, we can shape our world, no matter how chaotic it may seem.

INSIGHT INTO HOW WE SHOULD LIVE OUR DAILY LIVES

Let us remember that the symbols in Revelation are not mere events to be feared but rather a part of God's grand design that includes each of us. The question we are considering, "Because He is Governing the Cosmos, How Do I Live in This World?" reminds us that we are not alone in this journey and that we can trust in his divine governance over all things.

The passage from the book of Revelation is a powerful reminder of God's majesty and power. As women of faith, we are called to contemplate the depths of his sovereignty and consider how we can live meaningful lives under his rule.

Our faith in God's sovereignty should not be a passive acceptance of his authority but an active and deliberate choice to trust in his plan. We must hold fast to this belief, even in the face of the challenges and complexities of modern life. By doing so, we can navigate this world with confidence and purpose.

THE MESSAGE FOR WOMEN OF FAITH

As women, we have unique roles to play in God's plan. We are called to be caretakers, nurturers, and guides for those around us. We must use our gifts and talents to serve others and bring glory to God.

In sum, the message from Revelation should inspire us to live our lives with intentionality and purpose. By trusting in God's sovereignty and using our talents to serve others, we can find true fulfillment and meaning in our journey of faith.

It can be challenging to grasp the idea of God being in complete control of the chaotic events portrayed in this text. However, despite all the turmoil, we can see signs of divine order. For example, a vast star called Wormwood fell from the sky when the third angel sounded his trumpet. This led to the contamination of water sources and the loss of many lives. But it's important to note that this wasn't just a random occurrence. It happened precisely when the angel blew his trumpet, which was all part of God's plan.

Life can sometimes feel like it is spinning out of control, leaving us overwhelmed and stressed. This can be especially true for women juggling multiple responsibilities at home, work, and in the community. You might also be dealing with health issues or taking care of a sick loved one, in addition to the challenges that come with motherhood or a demanding job. However, in these moments, it's important to remember that you are not alone.

Like the great star under God's control, even though its impact was terrifying, your chaos is also under his control. He sees all the intricate details of your life and is there to help you navigate the storm. So take a deep breath, trust in his plan, and remember that your chaos is his canvas.

The idea of divine limitations amidst apocalyptic chaos is a powerful one. "They were told not to harm the grass of the earth or any green plant or any tree, but only those people who do not have the seal of God on their foreheads" (Rev. 9:4). When the fifth angel blew his trumpet, demonic locusts swarmed the earth. However, these locusts had specific restrictions; they were commanded not to harm the natural world or those who bore God's seal. The key lesson here is that God-imposed limitations exist even during our most difficult trials in life.

As women, we often feel like our trials have no end. The exhaustion of balancing work, family, and personal life can make it seem like God has forgotten us. However, like the locusts had limitations, our trials also have boundaries. We are reminded that God imposes limits on our suffering and that our challenges are not a sign of divine neglect but a part of a trial with a divine purpose.

THE SEVENTH TRUMPET: CALL TO ALL BELIEVERS TO BE PREPARED FOR CHRIST'S RETURN

Toward the end of this passage, we learn that despite the terrifying events, many people did not turn to God for help. "The rest of mankind, who were not killed by these plagues, did not repent..." (Rev. 9:20). This is an alarming notion. Still, it illustrates a critical point: peace comes from trusting God's sovereignty, even when facing fear and chaos. Those who did not repent lacked that peace, even when the evidence of God's power was irrefutable.

As women, we often find ourselves as peacemakers in our families and communities. We are the shoulders to cry on and the providers of emotional support. But where can we find peace for ourselves? The answer is straightforward: we find peace in trusting God's sovereignty, even when the world seems to be falling apart.

As women in the Lord's church, we find our strength in trusting God's sovereignty. With the unwavering belief in his overarching plan, we face life's challenges with courage and determination. We persevere through trials, knowing that they have divine limitations, and we find peace in the certainty of God's control over everything that scares us. We are empowered to live our lives with purpose and grace through our trust in God's sovereignty.

We often hear about Proverbs 31 women, those virtuous individuals who seem to have it all together. But I believe that before a woman can embody that ideal, she must first be a Revelation 8-9 woman who navigates life's complex, often terrifying circumstances with an unwavering trust in God's sovereignty. She understands that no trial is too great and no chaos too overwhelming for God. Her strength is not her own but is drawn from her deep-rooted faith in God, who governs the cosmos.

As you step out into another week, month, or stage of life, remember that your strength as a woman of faith lies not in your ability to control circumstances but in your unwavering trust in the One who does. He is not just a spectator but the scriptwriter, director, and producer of this grand cosmic play. With all its joys, sorrows, and complexities, your life is not a string of random acts but a symphony he is composing. And in that symphony, each note has a place, no matter how discordant it seems.

My dear sisters, let us remember that the challenges and trials we face are not signs of God's absence but rather an affirmation of His presence. We are not alone in navigating these experiences because they are part of God's divine plan. As women of faith, we can find comfort in knowing that God governs the universe, and we can confidently face the world with unwavering trust in his sovereign rule, no matter what chaos and difficulties come our way. In a world that often feels out of control, we serve a God in complete control. And that makes all the difference.

Let's delve into the significance of trusting in God's sovereignty, which will allow us to tackle the challenges of our daily lives. We can embody virtues that will help us rise above earthly tribulations and lead fulfilling lives that please God.

During celestial events, the role of the altar is fascinating. "Then the angel took the censer and filled it with fire from the altar and threw it on the earth, and there were peals of thunder, rumblings, flashes of lightning, and an earthquake" (Rev. 8:5). Before any trumpets are blown, an angel takes fire from the altar and throws it onto the earth. The altar symbolizes God's presence, sacrifice, and purity. The fire, once part of divine worship, is now part of divine judgment. This serves as a reminder that the same God we worship on Sundays is actively involved in unfolding world events —even those that appear chaotic or disastrous.

Just as the fire from the altar symbolizes both worship and judgment, we, too, are called to a life of duality. As women, we often lead cultural shifts and societal changes, taking on roles as educators, mothers, caregivers, and leaders. Despite our active participation in worldly roles, we must never forget that our ultimate allegiance is to the divine. Living righteously amidst chaos means bringing the fire of the altar, the fire of God's presence, into every aspect of our lives. It means imitating Christ in our actions, words, and thoughts and becoming His ambassadors in a broken world.

As we saw in the text, the locusts were instructed to harm only those not sealed by God. It is remarkable that amid divine judgment, there is divine protection for those who are sealed, which is a testament to God's never-ending care for his people. As women of faith, we can apply the concept of God's protective seal to our daily lives. We often act as emotional, psychological, and even physical shields for our families, protecting our loved ones in many ways.

Being women of God in these times requires us to serve others selflessly, not only our immediate families but also our communities and even strangers. Living a righteous life means serving others and providing a protective "seal" to those in need through a kind word, a generous act, or a moment of our time. As we read in Galatians 5:13, "For you were called to freedom, brothers. Do not use your freedom as an opportunity for the flesh, but through love serve one another." In doing so, we embody God's protective, selfless love in a world that sorely needs it.

Despite facing terrible calamities, many people refused to turn away from their immoral ways. "The rest of mankind, who were not killed by these plagues, did not repent of the works of their hands nor give up worshipping demons and idols of gold and silver and bronze and stone and wood, which cannot see or hear or walk" (Rev. 9:20). This resistance to repentance is not just a past phenomenon. Still, it can be seen in our modern world. In today's society, where moral lines are continually blurred, it takes courage to stand up for what is right. As women of faith, we are called to live morally and to actively fight against immorality in all its forms. We may face judgment, persecution, or alienation, but we should not be afraid. We serve a God who controls the entire cosmos, and we can overcome any obstacle with him by our side.

APPLICATIONS IN THE LIVES OF CHRISTIAN WOMEN

So, what does it look like to live righteously in a chaotic world as a woman in the Lord's church? It seems like a life imbued with the altar's fire—a life committed to imitating Christ. It looks like serving others selflessly, offering them the love and protection that emanate from a relationship with God. And it means taking moral stands in a world that increasingly leans toward relativism and sin.

We often hear the saying that "well-behaved women seldom make history." However, the key to making a lasting impact is not about conforming to societal standards of behavior but rather being 'God-behaved,' according to his divine standard of righteousness. Living a life that is pleasing to God is bound to shake up history because it challenges the very foundation of worldly values and priorities.

Remember that your righteous living is a testament to a cosmic God in complete control. Just as he has orchestrated the grand celestial events that will one day culminate in his final victory, he has also produced your life as part of his divine plan. Living righteously amid chaos is not just a lofty ideal; it's a holy calling. As you step out to face another day, take courage from the truth that your righteous acts are earthly deeds and heavenly investments.

We've journeyed through trusting God's sovereignty and living righteously amid chaos. As we conclude today, let's explore how to build a legacy of faith that will enrich our lives and deeply influence those who follow us. This is especially crucial for us as women, who often serve as the moral and spiritual compasses in our families and communities.

Revelation provides a startling reminder that the world's powers and principalities are at play, aiming to unleash chaos and darkness. "And the fifth angel blew his trumpet, and I saw a star fallen from heaven to earth, and he was given the key to the shaft of the bottomless pit" (Rev. 9:1). If a fallen star can be given such influence, how much more should we, as daughters of the Most High God, wield our influence for good?

Our impact on others is often greatest in our homes, where we serve as mothers, daughters, wives, and sisters. In Proverbs 31, the mother takes care of her household and teaches her children to fear the Lord. By actively teaching and modeling Christ-like behavior, such as through bedtime prayers, Bible stories, or resolving conflicts within the family, we nurture faith and lay the foundation for a legacy of faithfulness. Our homes are where this legacy of faith often begins. Through these daily acts of devotion, we pass on a godly heritage to the next generation.

We read in Revelation 9:18, "By these three plagues a third of mankind was killed, by the fire and smoke and sulfur coming out of their mouths." This verse depicts a devastating outcome and reminds us of the severe impact our actions, symbolized here by "fire, smoke, and sulfur," can have on those around us. While this scripture focuses on destructive effects, let's think of the opposite: What kind of positive, life-changing impact could we have if we emitted not fire, smoke, and sulfur but love, grace, and truth?

As women in the Lord's church, we have many opportunities to strengthen faith in our communities. Some of these include leading Bible studies and youth groups and taking part in initiatives that promote godliness and reflect Christ's love for those suffering. Our faith becomes more meaningful when we step out of our comfort zones and reach out to those outside our immediate circles. These actions not only enrich our own faith journeys but also help to build a legacy of faith within our larger community.

Despite the mighty works of God, many will choose not to repent or turn toward God. "The rest of mankind, who were not killed by these plagues, did not repent of the works of their hands..." (Rev. 9:20). However, this should not deter us from our mission to pass on a legacy of faith. For every person who chooses not to accept the message, there might be another who does, and your influence can be the turning point for them.

Consider the stories of matriarchs such as Sarah, Rebekah, and Mary—each faced unique challenges but played a pivotal role in God's redemptive story. They passed on the baton of faith through their lineage, actions, and, in Mary's case, through her womb. Our responsibility is to prepare the next generation to take up this baton and run their race with endurance.

So, what does building a legacy of faith look like practically for women in the Lord's church? It means fostering faith at home through godly parenting and nurturing. It means extending this influence to our broader communities through acts of love and service. And it means preparing the next generation to take the baton and run their godly race.

We may not all be biblical matriarchs or prominent church leaders. Still, we have a role in this grand symphony of faithfulness. Each note we contribute—whether a comforting word, an act of kindness, or a life lived righteously—adds to a melody that spans generations.

As we conclude our journey through Revelation 8:6-9:21, let's carry the weight of this responsibility and privilege with us. Let's strive to be women who trust in a sovereign God, live righteously, and build enduring legacies of faith.

In a world filled with chaos, doubt, and despair, let us be the ones who stand out, who firmly believe that we can face the world not with fear but with faith. Let us be the ones who live righteously amid chaos, not as an act of resistance but as an expression of our deep-rooted faith. And let us be the ones who pass on this faith, ensuring that our legacy will continue to glorify God long after we have run our course.

The legacy we build will be a testament to a God who is not only in control of cosmic events but is also intimately involved in the details of our lives. May your legacy point unmistakably to him, resonating with the melody of faithfulness for generations to come.

It is essential to reflect on how these profound truths should not just be discussion topics but woven into our daily lives. They should influence our choices, ambitions, and legacies.

In this passage from Revelation, we have explored three central truths. Firstly, we have delved into the importance of trusting in God's sovereignty, even when we find ourselves in confusing and turbulent times. Secondly, we have examined the significance of living righteously amidst chaos and understanding that our daily choices matter eternally. Finally, we have considered the weighty and joyous responsibility of building a legacy of faith for the generations that will follow us.

As Christian women, we are continually faced with a world where many people choose not to repent, even in the face of dire circumstances. However, we are called to be a contrasting image by trusting God, living righteously, and investing in a lasting legacy of faith. These actions are not isolated from each other but form a complete and interconnected cycle. When we place our trust in God, we are empowered to live righteously, which helps us build a lasting legacy of faith. Investing in this legacy strengthens our trust in God, creating a beautiful, self-reinforcing cycle of faith. Ultimately, this cycle of faith becomes an unshakable foundation in an often unstable and uncertain world.

The Bible contains many stories about women who lived out powerful principles with admirable qualities. Consider Ruth, who placed her trust in God and left her homeland. Or Esther, who fearlessly risked her life to save her people. The Proverbs 31 woman is another example, embodying virtues such as trustworthiness, righteousness, and legacy-building. These women were vital not only by worldly standards but also in how God defines strength – with a foundation in faith and expressed through love, wisdom, and courage. Their stories continue to inspire people of all backgrounds and ages.

The book of Revelation contains vivid descriptions of apocalyptic scenes that can be overwhelming and frightening. However, it is essential to remember that he is still in control despite the chaos depicted in these scenes. Not only is he in control of the entire universe, but he is also in charge of our individual lives. Even when we face trials and tribulations in life, we can trust that God has a plan for each one of us. His plan offers hope and a promising future, even when circumstances appear bleak. It is essential to hold on to this truth, especially in difficult times, and to lean on God for guidance and strength as we navigate life.

QUESTIONS

1. What do trumpets symbolize? What other times were trumpets mentioned in the Bible?

2. What parallels do you notice between the trumpet judgments in Revelation 8:6-9:21 and the ten plagues in Exodus 7-12?

3. What sin(s) are you holding on to despite warnings, rebukes, and perhaps consequences? Why?

4. The passage in Revelation 8:6-9:21 can be a fearful one, but only for the unprepared. How can we be prepared for the trumpet call, and for the turbulent times that come into each of our lives?

5. Woe, as used in Revelation 8:13, represents grief and God's broken heart over man's stubbornness. What is the spiritual root of stubbornness? Who in the Bible met his downfall due to his stubbornness?

Peggy Tidwell is Vice President of Commercial Banking at Park National Bank in Columbus, Ohio. She received her undergraduate degree from The Ohio State University and her Masters of Business Administration from Texas A&M University.

Peggy has served as President of Tri-Village Rotary, OSU Health Insights, and Commercial Real Estate Women (CREW Columbus). She was a founding member and Board member of Women for Economic and Leadership Development (WELD) and board/executive committee member of the Junior League of Columbus.

She currently serves as Chair of the Board of Trustees for Willow Brook Christian Communities, a continuous care retirement community in Central Ohio, and serves on the Board of Trustees for Freed-Hardeman University.

Her husband, Greg, currently is the pulpit minister for the Fishinger Road Church of Christ in Columbus, Ohio as well as the Editor of *Gospel Advocate*. Their twin sons, David and Jordan, both graduated from Freed-Hardeman University.

Because He Is Giving His Word, How Should I Receive It Willingly?

Revelation 10:8-10

Lacy Crowell

Twenty years ago my husband, Jonathan, and I decided to sell our home, pack up our two precious little ones and move halfway across the country from Oklahoma to Denver, Colorado to attend the Bear Valley Bible Institute and go into full-time ministry. As a lifelong preacher's kid I was confident I knew what we were getting into and I was excited, although nervous, about our new life. When my sweet mama asked to take me to lunch, just the two of us, right before we left, I knew she just wanted time with me and wanted to wish us well. I was wrong.

The next thing I knew I was sobbing in the middle of The Olive Garden. My mama loved me enough to tell me what I needed to hear, even though it definitely wasn't what I wanted to hear. By nature I am a people-pleaser extraordinaire. She knew that as

Christians, and especially in the ministry, there are times when you have to say hard things to people, and unfortunately it won't always go well. She looked me dead in the eyes and said the words I will never forget, "Lacy, not everyone liked Jesus himself. How dare you have the audacity to think everyone should like you." It hurt, but she was right and I needed to hear it. (God's sense of humor has never been more evident in my life than by the fact that I'm now Dean of Students at Freed-Hardeman University).

As Christians we love the Lord, and we love truth. Yet that truth can churn in our stomachs when we know that we have to say hard things to people. When we gently correct a misunderstanding of scripture, lovingly correct someone we love who is living in sin, or give someone bad news. This is the situation John finds himself in as we approach Revelation chapter 10, and we can learn a lot from the way John receives a difficult message from God.

> Then the voice that I had heard from heaven spoke to me again, saying, "Go, take the scroll that is open in the hand of the angel who is standing on the sea and on the land." So I went to the angel and told him to give me the little scroll. And he said to me, "Take and eat it; it will make your stomach bitter, but in your mouth it will be sweet as honey." And I took the little scroll from the hand of the angel and ate it. It was sweet as honey in my mouth, but when I had eaten it my stomach was made bitter. (Revelation 10:8-10) [All Scripture references are from the English Standard Version unless otherwise noted.]

This text is one of the amazing times when John actively interacts with the vision he is being given. Chapter 10 begins with incredible imagery: a mighty angel comes down from heaven, wrapped in a cloud with a rainbow over his head, his face like the sun, his legs like pillars of fire, and he places his right foot on the sea and his left foot on the land. The angel has a little scroll open in his hand, and he calls out with a voice like a lion roaring. In return seven thunders sound. As John is preparing to write down the message of the thunder, God tells him not to. Then the angel speaks. He raises his hand to heaven and swears by God that in the days of the trumpet call of the seventh angel the mystery of God would be fulfilled.

After the angel's incredible proclamation, in verse eight God specifically addresses John and tells him to take the scroll from the hand of the angel. Let's consider this briefly: This angel is so large that he is able to stand on both the land and the sea at the same time. His voice is so magnanimous that the thunders answer him. Yet John is not only to approach him, but speak to him and ask him for something.

I have been in some high-pressure situations that genuinely made me feel nauseous, but I can't even begin to fathom how John was feeling as he stared at this monstrous angel with the voice of God directly coming to him from heaven. To be honest I feel a little queasy at the idea of making a phone call, and I'm pitiful enough to pawn that off on my wonderful husband every chance I get. Picture in your mind what John is being asked to do here.

Amazingly, verse nine tells us that he went straight up to the angle and told him to give John the little scroll. For me, this begs the first practical question of our text: has God called us to do things that are intimidating? He hasn't asked us to approach a giant angel as he did John. He hasn't asked us to walk around naked as he did Isaiah (Isa. 20:2-4). He hasn't asked us to marry a prostitute as he did Hosea (Hos. 1:2). Yet there are certainly aspects of Christianity that are intimidating.

What is interesting is that what is intimidating for me may not intimidate you at all, and vice-versa. For example few things intimidate me as much as the idea of leading singing at a ladies' event. For my youngest daughter, Mya, it isn't a problem at all. She loves to lead singing but is incredibly intimidated at the idea of leading public prayer.

There's also so much more to this than public leadership. How do you feel about the idea of personal evangelism? What about actively mentoring and discipling a younger Christian? Teaching a teen girl's class? Teaching a children's Bible class? Do you struggle with what to say when writing cards? What about being willing lovingly to confront those who are in error as we discussed in the beginning?

In our service to the Lord there will always be areas we are more comfortable in than others. I believe there will also be areas we are more talented in than others. At the same time, I do *not* believe that a lack of comfort or talent is an excuse to sit idly by while a need in the Lord's church goes unmet. It is certainly not an acceptable reason to allow someone to remain in a lost state without even trying to reach them. We cannot let intimidating circumstances stop us any more than John could.

Continuing on in Revelation 10:9, after John asks for the scroll the angel speaks, "Take and eat it; it will make your stomach bitter, but in your mouth it will be sweet as honey." He is warned from the beginning that consuming God's word is not going to be entirely pleasant. In the last 2,000 years this has not changed.

Thinking back to the conversation I had with my mother, there are two points that specifically apply to our text. First of all, we need to love souls more than relationships. We need to love people enough to be willing to say what they need to hear even if it isn't what they want to hear. This is what agape love looks like in action.

In Luke 14:25-33 Jesus gives a clear and potent teaching regarding counting the cost of discipleship. In this text he teaches that he must come first above all our earthly family, and above ourselves. He teaches that being his disciple means daily bearing our own cross, and that we need truly to consider whether or not we are willing to do these things before we become a Christian.

I'm afraid we often skip this part when we are studying with people, and I'm afraid we skip it because we fear their answer will be "no." But note what Jesus says in Luke 14:27, "Whoever does not bear his own cross and come after me cannot be my disciple." He doesn't say it's difficult for them. He doesn't say it's unlikely. He says it's impossible. That means even if we get someone wet, if they have not counted the cost and determined to strive to put Jesus above all else, they are still not his child.

Christianity can be hard to swallow because there will be times when it costs us. In fact I would suggest that if our faith has never cost us anything, perhaps it's because there have been times we allowed other things, or other people, onto Jesus' throne.

One of the most heartbreaking statements I have ever heard was spoken to my husband and me early on in our ministry. We were working with a small congregation in a small town where the church had split years before. The congregations were working on reconciling, but the split had been over a doctrinal issue, so my husband and I had been studying with the individuals involved. My husband opened up scripture and read straight from God's word. The dear man we were studying with looked him dead in the eyes and said, "I used to believe it that way, until it affected someone I love." I immediately thought of the words of Jesus, "If anyone comes to me and does not hate his own father and mother and wife and children and brothers and sisters, yes, and even his own life, he cannot be my disciple," (Luke 14:26).

This is why Jesus' teachings on church discipline are so clear in Matthew 18:15-17. It is also why there are so many references to pruning and cleaning out the leaven. There are times when truth will cost us, and that is a very bitter pill to swallow. Yet for both our sake and theirs we must. The only chance we have of reaching those we love so dearly is to make sure they know that we love Jesus most, and that he loves them more than we ever could. Otherwise what are we trying to bring them to in the first place?

It's also why we need to be so mindful and protective of baby Christians. As with John, sometimes the truth starts out as honey and then turns bitter in our stomachs. For instance when we are so excited at the peace, healing, and joy we have found in Jesus and then those that we love most reject his teachings. When this happens we need to be sure to surround those baby Christians with love and encouragement to fill the gap of what they have lost with the love of Jesus.

Secondly, we need to keep this in mind when others love us enough to tell us what we need to hear, and hold us accountable. Keep in mind Proverbs 27:17, "Iron sharpens iron, and one man sharpens another." Picture this process in your mind, it requires both blades being hot, sparks flying, and both having their imperfections ground down. If we love like Jesus, we will never find pleasure or enjoyment in correcting someone else. If we do, we need to do a serious heart-check. But that also means that if someone loves us enough to come to us, it hurts them too. It costs them something too. Likely, God's truth has turned a little bitter in their stomach, and we need to respond in a way that respects their love and courage, even if their words hurt.

For our family, The Olive Garden has become a standing joke for the last two decades. If someone thinks they might be in trouble they say, "Uh-oh, are we going to The Olive Garden?!" Or when we actually do eat there its, "Watch out or Grandma will make you cry!" That's because my mama's love for me was never more clear than in that moment. Her wisdom and guidance allowed me to grow in a way that I desperately needed, and I genuinely don't think I would have made it in the ministry, and I certainly would not be able to fulfill my role as Dean, if she hadn't been willing to hold my short-coming up to scripture.

While sometimes God's word turns bitter in our stomachs because there is something hard that we need to do, there are other times that this discomfort is a sign of growth. Think about a runner who has just pushed themselves to the limit; oftentimes they will be holding their stomach because it hurts, and they may even feel nauseous. As Christians we are expected to grow, and with growth will inevitably come growing pains. Hebrews 5:12-14 says:

> For though by this time you ought to be teachers, you need someone to teach you again the basic principles of the oracles of God. You need milk, not solid food, for everyone who lives on milk is unskilled in the word of righteousness, since he is a child. But solid food is for the mature, for those who have their powers of discernment trained by constant practice to distinguish good from evil.

Have you heard the saying that there are individuals who have been Christians for 20 years, and there are those who have been first-year Christians 20 times? Being a first-year Christian 20 times is simply not pleasing to God. When we look back at the last year, or five years, how are we stronger in our faith now than we were? What are we doing now that we weren't doing then? How are the fruits of the Spirit (Gal. 5:22) manifested more in our lives now than they were? Who have we tried to share the incredible message of Jesus the Messiah with in that time?

While as women we are certainly not going to be preachers, I firmly believe that Paul's instruction to Timothy in 2 Timothy 2:2 still applies to us, "and what you have heard from me in the presence of many witnesses entrust to faithful men, who will be able to teach others also." As Christians we are to make disciple makers! Remember 1 Corinthians 3:6, "I planted, Apollos watered, but God gave the growth." We are not responsible for the hearts of others or their reaction to the gospel message, but, ladies, we better be out there sowing the seed!

I once heard it said that you don't truly understand something until you can explain it to a fifth grader. If we can't share the gospel plan we obeyed (Rom. 6), that's something we need to do some serious heart-searching about. Might it push us out of our comfort zone? Might it be scary, and even nausea-inducing? Absolutely. But once again if we are always comfortable, that's a pretty solid indicator that we are not growing.

Continuing on in Revelation 10, the angel has warned John that while the scroll will be honey in his mouth it will turn bitter in his stomach, and in verse 10 we see John's reaction to this warning, "And I took the little scroll from the hand of the angel and ate it. It was sweet as honey in my mouth, but when I had eaten it my stomach was made bitter."

Without hesitation John reaches out, takes the scroll from the gigantic angel and immediately consumes it. Continuing on in verse 11 this part of the vision comes to a close, "And I was told, 'you must again prophesy about many peoples and nations and languages and kings.'" John's reaction here calls to mind Isaiah's reaction in Isaiah 6:8, "Then I said, 'Here I am! Send me.'"

Knowing that the scroll was not going to be easy to consume; knowing that it would turn bitter in his stomach, John took it gladly and without hesitation. I believe he was able to do this for two primary reasons: first, because John truly loved God's word.

Rachel Robertson is a dear sister in Christ, and I had the privilege of hearing her speak this past fall at the Come Fill Your Cup Retreat. Rachel is a medical professional, and she shared some of her experiences from working in the oncology ward. She stated that one of the first ways they can tell when a patient is nearing the end of their life is when they lose their appetite. She stated that when they aren't hungry, they are dying. The same is true for us. If we don't hunger for God's word then we are spiritually dying.

Many feel that the idea of daily Bible reading is outdated, but if we can go an entire day without partaking of the bread of life and it doesn't affect us, we are not hungering and thirsting for righteousness (Matt. 5:6). God's word is the source of life, hope, joy, love, and peace. It's the ultimate source of wisdom to light our way. It shows us how to love and be loved, how to handle our painful emotions in a God-honoring way that brings growth and healing, and, most of all, how to be reconciled to him for eternity through the precious blood of Jesus. How can we not love and long for such richness in our daily lives!

What about in the lives of our families? Of our children and grandchildren? We would never dream of going an entire day without providing those precious babies physical food, are we as devoted to giving them spiritual food? Are we like the apostles, gone into town to buy physical food, or are we Jesus sharing the bread of life with the woman at the well? Are we Martha preparing the house, or are we Mary guiding our loved ones to the feet of Jesus? John received God's word willingly because he truly loved it, do we?

I also believe John was also able to receive God's word willingly because he loved souls. Verse 11 tells us that the scroll wasn't just for John's own nourishment, but he was expected to share it with others as well. The good and the bad, the sweet and the bitter, and we are expected to do the same. Think about the message John is receiving in Revelation. Ultimately it was a message of victory for the faithful; however remember the direct report he was to give to the seven churches of Asia, it was also a message of judgment for many. John gladly accepted God's commission to share both. Like Paul, he did not shirk from declaring the whole counsel of God (Acts 20:27), do we?

The story is told of a man who went down front after one of Penn and Teller's famous magic acts in Las Vegas to present Penn (famous for being an atheist) with a Bible. In a later interview Penn was asked if this made him angry. Penn's response was, "If you believe in heaven and hell, how much do you have to hate someone to not tell them?!" Sisters, the world is sick with sin and we have the cure! If we truly love people we will gladly receive God's word and share it with anyone who will listen.

"For the word of God is living and active, sharper than any two-edged sword, piercing to the division of soul and spirit, of joints and of marrow, and discerning the thoughts and intentions of the heart," Hebrews 4:12. Sometimes when we receive God's word it will be honey in our mouths, and sometimes it will turn bitter in our stomachs. Sometimes the struggle will be that there is something hard, a growth opportunity that we need to embrace. Sometimes the bitterness is a growing pain that will ultimately strengthen us as well as our example to those we love.

Either way it has been given to us to reprove, rebuke, and exhort each other (2 Tim. 4:2), so that we can "present [ourselves] to God as one approved, a worker who has no need to be ashamed, rightly handling the word of truth," (2 Tim. 2:15). Sisters, let us gladly receive the beautiful word of the Lord and share it will all who will listen.

QUESTIONS

1. Are there areas of Christianity that are intimidating to me? How can I work to grow in these areas?

2. What excuses do I tend to make when an area of Christianity makes me uncomfortable?

3. What hindrances in my life are keeping me from receiving the word gladly that I need to get rid of? If so, what are specific steps I can start taking to grow in this way?

4. What specific areas of spiritual growth have I been intentionally working on?

5. How do I react to scripture when it's hard? How can I intentionally work on having a soft heart that receives God's word willingly?

 **Lacy Crowell** is the Dean of Students at Freed-Hardeman University in Henderson, Tennessee. She has been married to the love of her life, Jonathan, for over 20 years. They are blessed with four amazing kiddos whom Lacy has had the privilege of homeschooling. She has also served alongside her husband in full-time ministry for 15 years.

Lacy loves to read, eat ice cream, and play Catan with her family (especially when she wins). She is a graduate of the Bear Valley Bible Institute of Denver and is a Licensed Marriage and Family Therapist. Her great joy is working to help her children and her sisters in Christ become excited about their service to the Lord and study of his word. She is a member of the Come Fill Your Cup team and the author of two Bible study books for women: *Proclaimed—Jesus the Messiah,* which is a study of the Gospel of Mark, and *Pursued—God's Plan for Intimacy in Marriage: a study of the Song of Solomon.*

Because He is Offering Hope, I Can Face Challenges
Revelation 11:11-18

Laurel Sewell
with Karen Sewell, Amy Sewell, and Holly (Sewell) McCall

"And the twenty-four elders who sit on their thrones before God fell on their faces and worshiped God, saying, 'We give thanks to you, Lord God Almighty, who is and who was, for you have taken your great power and begun to reign. The nations raged, but your wrath came, and the time for the dead to be judged, and for rewarding your servants, the prophets and saints, and those who fear your name, both small and great, and for destroying the destroyers of the earth.'" (Rev. 11:16-18)
[All scripture references are from the English Standard Version unless otherwise noted.]

God's word offers hope in meeting challenges in our relationships here on earth. One of the greatest challenges facing families is the relationship between in-laws, particularly between the mother-in-law and daughter-in-law. It was suggested that we have a panel discussion during our Freed-Hardeman Lectureship to give women a chance to voice their concerns and seek guidance from each other on this topic. This chapter is also in response to these concerns with suggestions on how to avoid pitfalls and to be proactive in establishing what can truly be a happy relationship.

"Pentheraphobia" is defined as the irrational fear or dislike of one's mother-in-law, causing long-lasting, intense physical and psychological reactions. Almost as fearful for some women, is the realization that she has suddenly been thrust into the role of the dreaded mother-in-law. Mary Tatem, in preparation for her book, *Just Call Me Mom*, surveyed 500 men and women across America, from newlyweds to great-grandparents, about their relationships and what makes them work or not work. She describes the realization that you, as a mother-in-law, are now "identified with that creature who is often scorned, despised, and the brunt of endless jokes. You know that every word you say will be weighed and possibly misunderstood by the new person in your family—the daughter-in-law" (Tatem 3).

In *Toxic In-Laws*, therapist Susan Forward identifies five types of personalities that may wreak havoc in families. They are the 'Critics' who target your worth as a person; the 'Engulfers' who expect you to spend all your spare time with them; the 'Controllers' who can't cut the ties with their child; the 'Masters of Chaos' who continually involve your family with their own family problems; and the 'Rejectors' who reject the in-law or even their own child in protest of their marriage (Forward 19). Fortunately, these represent the extremes, but there are lesser infractions that may cause problems for the married couple.

Why is this relationship between mothers-in-law and their daughters-in-law more problematic than between fathers-in-law and sons-in-law? There may be a rivalry for affection. Two women love the same man, in different ways, of course. And second, it is because you and your children have mutually exclusive goals:

- You want to maintain close relationships with your children. You long for meaningful contact with them and their spouses.
- Your grown children and their spouses want and need to separate themselves to establish their own family identity.

The harder you try to hold on, the harder they will pull away. But if you truly let go and allow them to have their freedom, they will return on their own. By using common sense, uncommon courtesy, and Biblical principles, those two mutually exclusive goals can be met.

BUILDING A PRAISE-WORTHY RELATIONSHIP

There are six basic needs of both the mother-in-law and the daughter-in-law. How can we help each other? Remember the obvious: not all women are alike. Some are mature. Some are immature. Some mothers-in-law will be trying to meet these needs and occasionally messing up, while others do not appear to be trying to get along at all. The same is true with daughters-in-law. Some genuinely want to get along, even though they may make occasional misjudgments. Others are not at all concerned with trying to get along, they just would rather you not be a part of the family.

From the reading I have done and from the answers to various questionnaires, it appears that most problems stem from violating one or more of these six general needs: *Privacy, Respect, Acceptance, Inclusion, Separateness, and Encouragement.* To build a *PRAISE-worthy* Mother-in-Law/Daughter-in-Law Relationship, let us use the acronym, PRAISE, to remind us of these needs.

Privacy

A daughter-in-law needs to maintain a measure of privacy from you. She does not appreciate prying questions. (When are you going to give me a grandchild? How many children are you going to have?) A daughter-in-law's home is not yours to decorate or manage unless she specifically asks for your help. She may have entirely different tastes from you. "Like a gold ring in a pig's snout is a beautiful woman without discretion" (Prov. 11:22).

Do not come for a visit without checking to see if it is an appropriate time. A mother-in-law and father-in-law also need privacy. They will appreciate grown children who consult the parents before coming for an extended stay. Find out if their coming would upset any plans they have made.

When calling on the phone, ask if it is a good time to talk, or if it is a busy time. Be willing to call back later, if necessary. Be considerate of her family's time.

Respect

A daughter-in-law wants respect from you. She will appreciate your compliments on her homemaking efforts. Remember you have more years experience than she does. She wants to feel competent in her role. Eliminate the feeling of competition. There is so much territory for a daughter-in-law and a mother-in-law to compare themselves with each other because they have many of the same jobs—cooking, housekeeping, child-rearing. By complimenting her abilities and being willing to learn from her in the things she does well, you take away the feeling of inadequacy.

She wants you to treat her husband (your son) as an adult also, not treating him like the little boy he once was. Do not 'baby' him. If we try to do too much for our adult children, we stifle their growth and keep them dependent on us. From the day your child is born, part of your job as a mother is to prepare yourself to be un-employed.

Do not give unsolicited advice. If they want your advice, they know where you live—they can come and ask for it. Realize they may or may not take that advice. Over-advising can backfire because it sometimes causes them to do just the opposite to pre-serve their independence.

Respect their time. Do not expect them to make plans that fit in with yours. They may not be able to come to all the extended family reunions. Do not put them on a guilt trip for it. "If possible, so far as it depends on you, live peaceably with all" (Rom. 12:18).

Learn to bite your tongue gracefully. Do not take sides in a disagreement between your son and daughter-in-law. That will make one of them feel outnumbered and frustrated. If the daughter-in-law feels that the mother-in-law and her husband are always a team against her, she will be angry with both of you, weakening the marriage bond as well as the mother-in-law-daughter-in-law bond. Nor is it good to side with your daughter-in-law over your son. He can begin to feel frustrated as well. It is best to remain neutral as possible. "Blessed are the peacemakers, for they shall be called sons of God" (Matt. 5:9).

A mother-in-law wants respect from you, the daughter-in-law. She will appreciate your compliments. She feels honored when you ask her how to do something. She wants to be valued by you. She wants to feel useful without feeling like she is being used. So, if you ask her to babysit, or do another act of service, be appreciative of any help you receive.

Try to see interference by the mother-in-law as a misguided attempt to be of help.

If it is unmanageable interference, one that is disrupting the harmony of your home, have a kind, frank discussion, and try to clear the air without creating a tornado.

Acceptance

A *daughter-in-law* wants acceptance as a person of worth. She may come from a different culture or background from you. She may have a different personality from you. She may have different opinions from you. She may even be of a different faith background from you. We must learn to accept people even when they are different from us. Overlook faults and weaknesses as you would want her to overlook yours.

A *mother-in-law* wants acceptance as a person of worth. There may be a difference in age, but do not disrespect that. She may come from a different culture or background from you but try to learn something from that difference. She may have a different personality from you. She may have different opinions from you. Learn to appreciate the differences between you and your in-laws.

With patience, a sense of humor, respect, and acceptance, you can overcome many background differences. "Above all, keep loving one another earnestly, since love covers a multitude of sins" (1 Pet. 4:8).

Inclusion

Most daughters-in-law want to be included as a member of the family. The daughter-in-law needs to know you value her as much as you value your son. Respondents to the survey by Mary Tatem mentioned how much they appreciated being given the same treatment as their husband's sisters when it came to gifts. One might perceive equality or inequality in the gifts that you give to her and to your son.

One fear that a mother-in-law may have is that of losing contact with her married children. The old saying, "A son is a son until he takes a wife, but a daughter is a daughter for the rest of her life," can be all too true. A mother-in-law wants to feel like family to you. She knows that she will not be a mother to you, for you have your own. But she does desire a good, loving relationship with you.

Thank her for bringing up the kind of son that you could love and respect. The mother-in-law needs to know that you appreciate the work she invested in rearing her son. Write her a nice note telling her how much you appreciate your husband, her son. Thank your daughter-in-law for caring for your son. Do not try to drive a wedge between your in-laws and their son. Remember that you will want to love, and be loved, by your own children even after they marry.

Separateness

Even more than inclusion in the family, the daughter-in-law also wants separateness for the family she and her husband are forming. These two needs seem opposite to each other, but both are necessary. Separateness may even be the most important need of all. God wants that for you also. "For this cause a man shall leave his father and his mother and shall cleave to his wife; and they shall become one flesh" (Gen. 2:24). I like to think of this as leaving, cleaving, and weaving you and your husband into the fabric of your own new family. Common transition points when in-laws are most vulnerable are the first meeting of the prospective in-laws; the wedding; and the addition of children-grandchildren to the family.

Be flexible. The parents-in-law should not expect things to remain the same as they were before the couple married. Be flexible in planning for holidays. Do not expect them to visit you as often as you might like. They need to establish their own friendships and connections.

Families must adjust expectations for holidays to make room for the daughter-in-law's family plans. Let her know that you want to collaborate with her to make sure she does not miss her own cherished traditions to fit into yours. Your family traditions might end—but some new ones will begin!

Separateness can be hard on the mother-in-law. The daughter-in-law who understands this can help ease the transition. As a mother with small children around your feet, you know just how those children are wrapped around your heart. You are interested in everything they do. You feel protective of them. You get some of your self-esteem and self-worth through your children. Then suddenly they are married and gone. The ties must be loosened. You cannot be involved in their daily life anymore. There is a sense of loss. But letting go of our adult children as we should, will bring blessings much greater than if we try to hold on to what we had.

In the book of Job, we see a similar experience with transition. Job had lost his children, not through marriage, but through death. Job's lament over the death of his children is, on a greater scale, like the loss of our adult children from our homes. To paraphrase, Job said, Oh, that I were as in months gone by... And my children were around me (from Job 29:2-5).

Transitions are hard. But in the last chapter of the book of Job we learn, "And the LORD blessed the latter days of Job more than his beginning..." and he saw "his sons, and his grandsons, four generations" (Job 42:12-17). When we look at our grandchildren, we realize that we received blessings that would not have been possible had we not let our children leave us.

The ability to anticipate and make transitions is a mark of maturity. We must anticipate and accept changes throughout life. The mother-in-law who has not anticipated the transition has set herself up for great disappointment when the transition takes place. We should anticipate that our children will one day leave our care, and we need to prepare them to take responsibility for themselves. We also need to prepare ourselves to be ready to let them go. This may come as a difficult task for some mothers-in-law, but it is vital to the success of her child's marriage. The mother who has spent her life sacrificing for her children has one more necessary sacrifice to make--she must let her children go.

A mother-in-law can accept this separateness more readily if she begins to develop herself in ways that are independent from her children. Remember, your son has limited free time from work, and that is the only time your daughter-in-law and their children have with him. Do not expect him to spend it all on you. Cut the apron strings. Your son and his wife are a unit. Treat them as one.

Be thankful to God that there is a woman who loves your son and wants to make him happy. We need to back out of their lives and let them become their own persons. The 'empty nest' gives you a chance to develop new interests that you may not had time for before. Learn a new skill. Dig into genealogy. Take a painting class. Keeping your body busy keeps you from being a busybody.

Encouragement

And the last of these six areas of needs is encouragement. Our married children want and need to make a success of their marriages. We can lend our moral support in encouraging that success. Mothers-in-law, praise your daughter-in-law to your son. Do not find fault with her cooking or her housekeeping or her child-rearing. She may be a novice at it. How you feel toward her will affect how your son sees her, and you want to promote his respect of her, not weaken it.

Remember, the way she feels toward you will color the way your son sees you throughout the rest of his life. Encourage the couple by being willing to serve them when they need it. They may need physical help in cleaning up a house they have just bought. When babies come, they may need your help. Be willing, but not insistent about helping. Financial assistance, without making them dependent upon you, can be most encouraging. A daughter-in-law appreciates a mother-in-law who stands ready to serve her family without taking over.

Pray for your daughter-in-law and son-in-law. They are, or may become, the parents of your grandchildren. You had influence over your own children – you could teach them to love God and to be mannerly, and you want the same for your grandchildren. But this is now in someone else's hands. Pray for your own relationship with your in-laws to grow. The in-law is a piece in the puzzle of your family now. Having your love, your son's love, and the love of the grandchildren is a blessing that makes all the struggle of raising children and letting them go seem worthwhile.

Be mature. Do not carry your feelings on your sleeve. Overlook trivial things that might bother you instead of dwelling on them. In kindness, work out any serious misgivings before they fester. Realize, no matter how hard you try, you will make mistakes, often without even being aware of it. Be quick to apologize when you realize your mistake.

If you have tried your best to be accommodating and loving, she will be more willing to forgive your blunders. Remember how you felt as a young wife with the new burden of responsibilities of a home, husband, and children and be ready to give grace. "Keep fervent in your love for one another because love covers a multitude of sins." (1 Pet. 4:8).

The greatest encouragement for a mother-in-law is to know that her son is loved and valued by his wife; or that her daughter is loved and valued by her husband; that they are providing a nurturing home, bringing up good children in a home that serves God. Nothing else really matters.

The following list appeared in a *Dear Abby* column in July of 2000. These 'commandments' help us to build a PRAISE-worthy relationship. Note: The words in parentheses are additions of mine.

Ten Commandments for a mother-in-law, by Iola M. Irwin.

1. Thou shalt love, honor, and respect the new couple. (*Respect, Inclusion*)

2. Thou shalt allow them complete independence. (*Separateness*)

3. Thou shalt speak only kindly and loyally about them. (*Respect*)

4. Thou shalt not find fault. (*Acceptance*)

5. Thou shalt not visit them too frequently, and never enter their home without knocking. (*Privacy*)

6. Thou shalt not expect them to visit you too often. (*Separateness*)

7. Thou shalt not give advice unless requested. (*Respect, Separateness*)

8. Thou shalt not mention how much you look forward to grandchildren. (*Privacy*)

9. Thou shalt respect their taste in home decorating, though it differs from your own. (*Respect, Acceptance*)

10. Thou shalt petition daily the Heavenly Father, in whose love they abide, for their happiness. (*Encouragement*)

In all our relationships, the inspired words from the Bible are the best advice anyone could receive. This is where we receive our hope. The apostle Peter quotes from Psalm 34 when he writes:

Finally, all of you, have unity of mind, sympathy, brotherly love, a tender heart, and a humble mind. Do not repay evil for evil or reviling for reviling, but on the contrary, bless, for to this you were called, that you may obtain a blessing. For whoever desires to love life and see good days, let him keep his tongue from evil and his lips from speaking deceit; let him turn away from evil and do good; let him seek peace and pursue it. For the eyes of the Lord are on the righteous and his ears are open to their prayer. But the face of the Lord is against those who do evil. (1 Pet. 3:8-12)

QUESTIONS

1. Study carefully each phrase in I Peter 3:8-12. How might these admonitions improve the in-law relationship—indeed, any relationship?

2. How can one strike a balance between inclusion and separateness?

3. How can a mother-in-law foster good sister-in-law relationships between her daughters-in-law and her own daughters?

4. As a daughter-in-law, what do you need and want for your family life? What can you do to help you achieve your own needs and wants without interfering with the mother-in-law's needs and wants?

5. As a mother-in-law, what do you want and need for your family life? What can you do to help you achieve your own needs and wants without interfering with the daughter-in-law's needs and wants?

6. What will you do to encourage your in-laws?

7. Read Colossians 3:12-14. Discuss how this relates to the in-law relationship.

8. As students of the Bible, we are familiar with Ruth and her mother-in-law, Naomi. After Ruth's remarriage to Boaz, do you remember who was Ruth's second mother-in-law? See Matthew 1:5 and Ruth 4:10-22.

BIBLIOGRAPHY

Forward, Susan. *Toxic In-laws. Loving Strategies for Protecting Your Marriage.* New York, N.Y. HarperCollins Publishers, 2001.

Tatem, Mary. *Just Call Me Mom! Practical Steps to Becoming a Better Mother-in-law.* Camp Hill, Pennsylvania: Christian Publications, 1994.

 **Laurel Shannon Sewell** is a graduate of Mars Hill Bible School and the University of North Alabama, in Florence, Alabama. Laurel and her husband, Milton, have been married for 58 years. Their family includes two sons, Scott Sewell and his wife Amy; Shannon Sewell, his wife Karen, daughter Holly and her husband John McCall and six grandchildren.

Laurel served as First Lady of Freed-Hardeman traveling and speaking on behalf of Christian education while her husband served as President for 18 years and currently while he serves as Chancellor. She is the author of *The Six Gifts of Hospitality*, a ladies' Bible class study book, and has contributed articles for several Christian publications.

Because He is Victorious Over Evil, I Can Win Over Sin
Revelation 12:7-12

Meagan Spencer

R
evelation can be somewhat strange when read as a type of novel or biography. Revelation is God making relevant truths known to man (Nave 1990). What Revelation reveals is an art gallery; harrowing feats with sweeping landscapes emerge around every corner on the walls of heaven. A narrative continues to be told out of the works of art that only God can create; in this grand narrative, though evil continually threatens God's work, God prevails. The people start to worship things other than God, and this is a reminder to think about where we place our choices because, ultimately, who we choose and our choices are worship or a rendering to God and thanksgiving that both reflect adoration to whom or what is the focus (Nave 1990).

Revelation, the art gallery, demonstrates that we have a choice in what we worship, in what we are thankful for, and these together form our ultimate adoration. Read Revelation 12:7-12.

Then war broke out in heaven: Michael and his angels fought against the dragon. The dragon and his angels also fought, but he could not prevail, and there was no place for them in heaven any longer. So the great dragon was thrown out -- the ancient serpent, who is called the devil and Satan, the one who deceives the whole world. He was thrown to earth, and his angels with him. Then I heard a loud voice in heaven say. The salvation and the power and the kingdom of our God and the authority of his Christ have now come, because the accuser of our brothers and sisters, who accuses them before our God day and night, has been thrown down. The conquered him by the blood of the Lamb and by the word of their testimony; for they did not love their lives to the point of death. Therefore rejoice, you heavens, and you who dwell in them! Woe to the earth and the sea because the devil has come down to you with great fury, because he knows his time is short. [All Scripture references are from the Christian Standard Bible unless otherwise noted.]

In this depiction, the beast or Satan is our captor, but what other captors hold us? The line is best described as a chain of expectation, a chain of bondage through time. When will we break the chains of the past? Breaking these chains starts with who we follow and the choices that we make. What does the battle of Revelation 12:7-12 behold?

Art comes in the form of literature, as well. God is justice and Christ is mercy; therefore, there is consequence to not following God, yet mercy for turning to him (Lewalski). Revelation 12:7-12 demonstrates a present destruction and justice of God kicking Satan out of the heavenly realm with a future promise of mercy and Christ kicking Satan out of the earthly realm. However, is this the earthly apocalypse or that of heaven?

Currently housed in the Cleveland Museum of Art, Albrecht Durer's 1511 woodcut, St. Michael fighting the Dragon, part of his Revelation of St. John series of fifteen scenes from the apocalypse, depicts this moment in Revelation 12:7-12. We see in this scene that God has the final say, the final victory! Digging deeper, these words should not be unfamiliar with previous scripture in both the old and new testaments, as the bible is a connected and continual narrative reflected in the Father, the Son, and the Holy Spirit through the Word. We see revelation of both the power of heaven and the choices that we make in the Father in Exodus 14:14, "The Lord will fight for you, and you must be quiet."

And then in the words of the Son in Matthew 22:37-38, "He said to him, Love the Lord your God with all your heart, with all your soul, and with all your mind. This is the greatest and most important command. The second is like it: Love your neighbor as yourself. "

So, when did or when will this apocalyptic resolution occur? Well, it already has. We start seeing the foreshadowed victory of Christ within this Revelation passage and all the way back in one of the oldest books of the bible, the book of Job.

Currently housed in the Tate London, William Blake's 1825 work, The Fall of Satan depicts a detour of end times, but again, are we discussing worldly end time or a final victory explanation of the blood of Christ?

Blake's work comes from the same Revelation scene of Durer, yet a different biblical passage. Blake paints a critical stage from the book of Job. We see the fall of Satan; however, there is suggestion that Satan was still able to accuse humanity before God in heaven until the final blow of victory in ultimate sacrifice, ultimate blood in Christ that throws Satan to his entire eviction out of heaven. Under the law of Moses, blood was temporary in sacrifice. Sins were atoned with the blood of animals, but that atonement had to start all over again after each sacrifice; therefore, it is suggested that while Satan was thrown out of heaven during the days of Job, he may have had temporary access to heaven to accuse because of the temporary atonement system. Blood was consecrated, or prayed over and requested to make holy in the name of God. However, Jesus' blood that is permanent would keep Satan from accessibility of accusation because we will be continually covered in his consecrated blood and even Satan recognizes the holy and must bow down before it, as is reiterated in James 2:19, "You believe that God is one. Good! Even the demons believe—and they shudder."

There was not a doubt that Satan and the rest of the fallen angels, now demons, recognize the holy and when there is consecrated blood, there is no accusation because the debt record is no more. As Colossians 2:14 states, "he erased the certificate of death, with its obligations, that was against us and opposed to us, and has taken it away by nailing it to the cross."

The debt record contained legal demands. That record was nailed to the cross and this is said repeatedly in the past foreshadowing prophecies of the Old Testament and present and future confirmation of both Jesus and the apostles in the New Testament. Psalm 103:12 states, "As far as the east is from the west, so far has he removed our transgressions from us."

This is the significance of the battle that we now come to in Revelation 12:7-12. Let's dig into this particular section of Revelation 12:7-12 verse by verse.

REVELATION 12:7

Where have we seen Michael? In Daniel 10:12-21 and 12:1. Michael is seen as a guardian angel of Israel. These verses in Revelation shadow Daniel showing that there is nothing new under the sun and that the biblical narrative will ultimately come together.

J. B. Coffman states that this is not a use of pagan mythology to understand versions of truth and future apocalyptic occurrences, but this is about past events and can be taken fairly literally in the sense that parables can, with some cultural symbolism used to understand the events that have happened and why they matter. Otherwise it would contradict the gospels (Beckwith; Coffman).

REVELATION 12:8

The accusation relay between heaven and earth that we see happen after the fall of Satan from heaven, which we also find in Job 1:6-12, is now done. There is not an accuser with the blood of Christ literally dripping from the cross and metaphorically from our faces as we put on the blood of Christ in baptism. Christ's authority is proclaimed in heaven and earth and to the saints that are now in his kingdom.

Here we see the set up for verse 10 that we are predestined for glory but must choose glory. We are predestined in that all events are willed by God, yet it does not paradox freewill because we still choose who we will serve and whether we accept these events (Lookadoo). We know that "his rule is not accepted by many, due to the freewill of man; but that does not contradict the higher truth that Christ is truly reigning today in the hearts of those who love and serve him" due to the presence of the holy spirit come from heaven (Coffman 265; Hendriksen).

REVELATION 12:9

The term "devil" means slander and "Satan" has similar origins as it means deceiver and accuser (Nave; Walvoord). The devil loves to discredit Christians (Nave; Walvoord) He is not red and horned; he deceives with beauty and good without God (Nave; Walvoord) Therefore, when an action seems good it may be, but we need to ask: Is it kingdom worthy? This verse is a warning that Satan is stealthy and will take his wrath out on mankind, so we must choose what we will listen to, what choices we will make (Coffman; Thomas). How do we make good choices and gain wisdom and discernment? In academia, researchers use a process of triangulation to check data. Triangulation makes sure everything is verified through at least a three-point process. This is a helpful tool to use when met with a questionable situation. The triangulation process for Christians includes scripture, prayer, and accountability. First, the word of God reveals truth just as we see in the example of Jesus. How do we know we are interpreting that truth correctly? Second, we go to God in prayer that the Holy Spirit will provide wisdom and discernment of the situation just as we see in the example of the New Testament church. Third, we build intergenerational relationships in the church and find those who are well studied and make wise and discerning choices as we see in the example of the New Testament church.

This is how we use our choices and strength in God to discredit the slanderer through communication and action. During the fall, Jesus also became our interceder, meaning that we now have a direct communication line with God (Coffman; Thomas). This direct communication line becomes a powerful tool in discrediting Satan's falsification.

With Christ as our interceder, we can use prayer as a tool to defeat slander and deceit. This is especially important as we see the transition of the law of Moses to the Christ's death. Hebrews 9:11-15 reiterates that the consecration of blood staves off sin and rebellion, and keeps Satan away from condemning us which reflects why this battle in Revelation after the death of Christ is so important. Hebrews 9:16-22 further connects the necessity of consecration and recognizing the holy by describing Jesus as mediator and calling us to live in his light, to make the choice of who we will serve and reflect.

So why doesn't God just end it all? Why does he allow bad, why does he allow testing? In this verse we see evidence that angels also have freewill. If we don't have freewill, we are slaves and God's love is not rooted in selfishness just as he wants us to model our relationships, we are made in the image of God. God's intention was not the Huxley's Island or Plato's Republic. We develop grit, that resilience in the face of trial, showing where our true loyalties lie just as Job did. His intention has never been a utopian manifesto. Utopias are static, void of relationship or growth, because they are just clockwork. So why would God create something that he couldn't have a relationship with? Do we, likewise, want a child that we just watch, but don't talk to, shout joyfully for when they hit a home run, and find pride in teaching (Lookadoo)?

Back to our art gallery. Blake's depiction of Job is a rising action to the gospel's climax of Christ's death, and Revelation's epilogue, or John's conclusion of what has happened and why it matters.

Why was this grand battle fought in the first place? Satan thought he could somehow prevent the resurrection and glorification of the Lord (Coffman).

Paul confirms this further in Ephesians 6:12 that this is a great spiritual battle of truth versus deception, "For our struggle is not against flesh and blood, but against the rulers, against the authorities, against the cosmic powers of this darkness, against evil, spiritual forces in the heavens."

Both John and Paul encourage Christians to recognize this battle between fear and faith.

REVELATION 12:10

We come to the glory of worship or confirmation of the nature of God, who he is, his power. Satan can do damage in the world as humans can because we see that he has a certain amount of free will just as we do, causing his fall and ours as humans. Where a record of debt was kept before for temple sacrifice to cover, this record is no more. The accusations are gone. Paul mentions this in Romans 8:33-34, "Who can bring an accusation against God's elect? God is the one who justifies. Who is the one who condemns? Christ Jesus is the one who died, but even more, has been raised; he also is at the right hand of God and intercedes for us." The sin was stripped out of our hands and into the nails of Christ's hands. Satan was robbed of the condemnation. Jesus then became our intercessor and advocate as we reflect to that proclamation in Hebrews 7:25,

"Therefore, he is also able to save completely those who come to God through him, since he always lives to intercede for them."

The revelation of what will happen has caused the battle; then the fulfillment of promise happens. In verse 10, Christ's resurrection victory makes this event theologically impossible to be post-resurrection because Christ reigns in victory defeating death.

REVELATION 12:11

Two things defeated the accuser, both Jesus' blood and testimony or evidence of his love for us as is also confirmed in Hebrews 9:14 (Nave), "how much more will the blood of Christ, who through the eternal Spirit offered himself without blemish to God, cleanse our consciences from dead works so that we can serve the living God?" Spurgeon states that "these saints used the doctrine of atonement not as a pillow to rest their weariness, but as a weapon to subdue their sin" (*Lectures*) This putting on of blood or baptism is in each choice we make, not defensive in only a selfish act of protection. When we become Christians, we are baptized in consecration of his blood and have the testimony of Jesus to share. How has the power of Christ despite the evil of Satan, the sins of people, the degradation of earth due to the entrance of sin enveloped in our narratives?

REVELATION 12:12

What is your narrative? What is your story? We get an artwork of victory in Christ with our narratives as well! Is it messy? Welcome to being a real person! Have you messed up? Welcome to God's grace! Have you had to walk away from everything? Jesus warned us of that. Is the pain, grief, and joy worth it? In Christ, yes, always. We see the truth of sin when we see the hideousness of death. "Satan makes sin seem pleasurable, but the cross reveals its bitterness. If Jesus died because of sin, men begin to see that sin must be a murderous thing." (Spurgeon, *Sermons*).

The amazing thing is that nothing is contradicted, and everything revealed can be applied to past, present, and future. Christ is victor, and following God is relatively simple. Micah 6:8 reiterates: "Mankind, he has told you what is good and what it is the Lord requires of you: to act justly, to love faithfulness, and to walk humbly with your God."

We must choose to live and speak the victory of Christ in our narratives. What is your story? Often our stories happen in the compilation of subtle events in which, when reflected upon, we find the immense glory of God. Sound familiar? Sound like a biblical narrative?

I would not be a Christian if it were not for these subtle events. Some of you may not know that I was adopted as an adult. My childhood consisted of the turmoil of physical, mental, and sexual abuse from my biological family. I would do just about anything to find "safe." A girl at school invited me to her youth group, and her parents even picked me up, such a small thing that started changing the entire trajectory of my life. I do know that there were so many subtle things that occurred that make the beautiful body of Christ, his church. Forever in my mind is seared the image of every person who did what they could from letting me sleep at their house, to giving me their children's old clothes, to letting me borrow a car to go to work, and the list goes on. I would end up homeless, not having an emergency contact to even write down; going to college with a friend just to escape my situation. Thanksgiving rolled by and again God struck in a small phone call asking if I would like to stay with a family; and I did each holiday off. I absolutely know that my parents will read this embarrassed that I mention this because they did not act out of "saviorism" but out of the genuine love of Christ and if you have adopted a child, especially an older child, I know you feel the same. Once again, the entire trajectory of my life was changed. At age 24, I came back to Tennessee with their encouragement and the encouragement of the church, and again God struck in the subtle question of if I would like to be adopted, and the narrative of God shapes us to His glory and continues. That is just a tidbit. Though there may be evil, though you may lose everything, God, and our choice to choose him work together to reflect the valleys and peaks of the biblical narrative. They reflect victory no matter what happens. It is not always pretty; there are many ugly parts to it; there will be loss and grief. Butlet us not downplay the difficulty, or think that we are immune to any other earthly woes. However, I am so thankful for a church that believes that Jesus defeats evil; a church that has seen the ugly yet thought with conviction of the blood of Christ in this battle that a person was worth both love and action. That is my testimony, and that paired with the blood of Christ in baptism is my beautiful artwork of what was to come out of Revelation 12:7-12. Michael's banishment of Satan, Christ's victory over Satan, and our choices over Satan. The beautiful revelation of salvation.

Spurgeon states this amazing victory the best when he writes,

First, you are to regard Satan this day as being already literally and truly overcome through the death of the Lord Jesus. Satan is already a vanquished enemy. By faith grasp your Lord's victory as your own, since he triumphed in your nature and on your behalf... Come, my soul, thou hast conquered Satan by thy Lord's victory. Wilt thou not be brave enough to fight a vanquished foe, and trample down the enemy whom thy Lord has already thrust down? Thou needest not be afraid, but say, "Thanks be to God which giveth us the victory through our Lord Jesus Christ." (1888)

This was a demonstration of the ultimate love that Paul describes in Romans 5:8, "But God proves his own love for us in that while we were still sinners, Christ died for us."

Satan is defeated, death is no more.

QUESTIONS

1. How do different works of art depict the battle between Michael and the dragon as described in Revelation 12:7-9?

2. What symbols or imagery do various artists use to represent the celestial conflict?

3. In what ways does art capture the intensity and magnitude of spiritual warfare?

4. How do artists convey the victory of Michael and his angels over the dragon in their heavenly battle?

5. What emotions or feelings does this passage evoke in you as you contemplate the cosmic struggle portrayed in Revelation 12:7-12?

6. How does this battle relate to the overall theme of spiritual warfare in Revelation?

7. How does this event contribute to our understanding of Satan's role in human history and his ongoing influence on the world?

BIBLIOGRAPHY

Beckwith, Isbon T. *The Apocalypse of John*. Wipf and Stock, 2001.

Coffman, James Burton. *Commentary on Revelation*. Firm Foundation, 1979.

Hendriksen, William. *More than Conquerors: An Interpretation of the Book of Revelation*. Baker, 1998.

Lewalski, B. K. *Paradise Lost and the Rhetoric of Literary Forms* (Vol. 186). Princeton UP, 2014.

Lookadoo, Jonathan. *A Commentary on the Revelation of John*, George Eldon Ladd, Eerdmans, 2018, 308 pp., pb 30. *Reviews in Religion and Theology*, 26(3), 458-460.

Nave, Orville J. *Nave's Topical Bible*. Hendrickson, 1990.

Spurgeon, Charles H. *Lectures to My Students*. United Kingdom: Passmore and Alabaster, 1875.

- - -.*The Metropolitan Tabernacle Pulpit: Sermons*. United Kingdom: Passmore and Alabaster, 1856.

- - -. *The Metropolitan Tabernacle Pulpit*. United Kingdom: Passmore, 1888.

Thomas, Robert L. *Revelation Exegetical Commentary* - 2 Volume Set. United States: Moody, 2016.

Walvoord, John and Philip E. Rawley. *Revelation*. Moody, 2011.

Dr. Meagan Spencer is the Director and an Assistant Professor of the Freed-Hardeman Communication Sciences and Disorders Program. She also serves as the President-Elect and VP of Communications of the TN Association of Audiologists and Speech Pathologists. Meagan resides in Henderson, Tennessee and is a member of the Estes Church of Christ.

Because He is Preparing to Judge, I Can Live a Holy Life

Revelation 13-14

Rita Cochrane

Now that you have reached chapter 13 in Revelation, most likely you have discovered its uniqueness. It is the Omega of scripture, but it is also a book we might shun due to its perplexing prophecy and imagery. In truth, Revelation seems to have jumped straight off the screen of a sci-fi movie. Although the chapters and verses of this curious book cause us some confusion, its overall theme is simple:

Life can be a battle, but in the end, mighty God wins!
Remain faithful!

If you love a story with a happy ending, just know as we jump into the book of Revelation, we must wade through the difficult before discovering our "happily ever after."

REVELATION 13

A Dragon and Two Beasts

Before we read Revelation chapter 13, you might want to take a moment to read Ephesians 6:10-18 [All scripture references are from the New King James Version unless otherwise stated.] and dress yourself in the armor of God because you will discover all eighteen verses filled with scary imagery. Two frightful beasts appear. One rises from the sea and the other from the earth, and both hold great power over all humankind. And if that isn't scary enough, their great power is fueled by a fierce dragon.

The dragon

Our introduction to the dragon came in chapter 12 and we do not need to guess his identity. Revelation 12:9 tells us that the dragon is the serpent we met in Genesis and is "called the Devil and Satan, who deceives the whole world."

The dragon was named Lucifer by the prophet Isaiah. Lucifer's plan was to "ascend into heaven" and "be like the Most High" (Isa. 14:13-14). Sadly, this Lucifer has never abandoned this plan throughout the ages.

The beast from the sea

The first scary beast arrives from the sea and possesses the qualities of fierce animals. It is swift like a leopard, has the strength of a bear, and the mighty roar of a lion. Such are the images from which nightmares are made. However, as scary as the beast may seem, its true horror lies in its audacity to blaspheme God (Rev. 13:1 and 5-6).

When was the last time you considered the seriousness of blasphemy toward God? Simply put, when contempt for the sovereignty of Holy God is expressed though our words and actions, this is blasphemy. Or, when someone elevates their worth, or any other worth, above the majesty of the creator and ruler of the universe, blasphemy has taken place.

The first beast is blasphemous twice. Look at Revelation 13:1 and 5-6, and you will discover the misguided thoughts the beast holds concerning its power. Yes, the beast is mighty, but its power cannot compare to God's. The beast is seen blaspheming God's name, God's tabernacle, and all those who dwell with God. His blasphemy was a sin scriptures says evades forgiveness (Matt. 12:31). Why? Because to receive forgiveness, sinful hearts must confess and forsake the sin. Repentance comes from a humble heart and from acknowledging God's sovereign majesty. Proverbs 23:12 confirms this with "He who covers his sins will not prosper, but whoever confesses and forsakes them will have mercy." Until Satan confesses and forsakes his sin, his blasphemy will remain unforgiveable. Oh, dear friend, how dangerous it is to hold onto a blasphemous heart.

The beast from the earth

To add to this nightmare, a second scary beast enters John's vision. This one comes from the earth, and his appearance, too, is frightful. His voice is as the voice of the dragon. He spreads blasphemy as he calls down fire from heaven. In Revelation 13:12 we see this beast "causes the earth and those who dwell in it to worship the first beast." Beast number two tells all the earth to "make an image to the beast who was wounded by the sword and lived" (Rev. 13:14). Where there is instruction to create an idol and worship it, this is blasphemy, for God alone is to be worshipped and adored.

Their identities

We have established Satan's identity to be that of a dragon. It's easy to imagine Satan breathing down fire with anger. But what about the two beasts? Most scholars agree that the beast from the sea represents the empires or political systems of the world, whereas the beast from the earth represents the religious kingdoms of the world. Sadly, chapter 13 reveals that both systems are under the rule of the dragon, possessing his great power. These institutions persecuted Christians as John wrote this revelation from God.

Friend, stop just a moment to consider our world today. Could we, too, discover a political system that has to a great degree departed from God's sovereign will? Might we, too, see numerous ways religious groups have left the teachings of the Word of God? Revelation was written long ago to a world in chaos, but we cannot overlook how we, today, stand in a similar place. Without a doubt, Christians are called to remain steadfast in the Word of God and disciple others by living holy lives that shine like stars (Phil. 2:15) and expose Satan for who he truly is.

Christians reading through chapter 13 feel an overwhelming sense of gloom and doom portrayed by the two beasts and powerful dragon. Perhaps this chapter was rightly numbered 13, because a most unlucky situation is portrayed through a sense of hopelessness. But we must remember, with God, things are never hopeless. "With God, all things are possible" (Matt. 19:26). So, we must not stop here because the next chapter will deliver a vision of hope we do not want to miss.

REVELATION 14

The Lamb

If chapter 13 left you stressed out, take a deep cleansing breath, because the "Lamb standing on Mount Zion" (Rev. 14:1) appears, and just like that, beasts and dragons take a back seat. Peacefulness enters John's vision, and we discover welcomed tranquility in chapter 14.

Following the dragon and beast nightmare, it is easy to imagine John's sigh of relief as he looked up and saw this Lamb on Mount Zion surrounded by a multitude of believers. Hebrews 12:22 tells us "Mount Zion" is "the city of the living God, the heavenly Jerusalem," and is filled with God's angels. What a welcome scene!

We find the sights and sounds of chapter 14 in sharp contrast to the previous chapter. John hears the voice of God. It is both as peaceful as the sound of water and as powerful as thunder all at the same time. Perhaps John considered how God offers both peace and power. Was John immediately filled with peace knowing powerful God was in control? We, too, can feel the peace that comes from knowing our powerful God is in control.

Next, John hears a melodious symphony of harps as they accompany the songs of the redeemed. They sing a new song as they stand faultless before the throne of God. Surely, John was grateful for this mood-shift in his vision, for what he saw and heard was sweet and soothing to his soul.

The Redeemed

Redeemed! What a precious word. Those who sang the new song before the throne were "redeemed from the earth" (Rev. 14:3). To be redeemed means to be brought back to God after sin has separated us from His Holy Presence. Because of his great love, God purchased us with an unspeakable price, and we can stand faultless before him. Take just a moment to allow this unfathomable concept to soak in. Are you still confused by unfathomable redemption? Here's a story that might help.

My doorbell rang and there, on my porch, stood a gentleman unfamiliar to me. Curiously, his purpose in stopping by lay discarded in our ditch. You see, several weeks prior, a large walnut tree had fallen in our yard and out by the road now lay a mountain of decaying tree parts awaiting rubbish pick-up.

The man's request was simple: He desired some of our discarded wood. I found myself amused by his courtesy, because, let's face it, when was the last time I refused to let someone haul off my trash? He thanked me for the "gift" and left me standing at the door puzzled over his gratitude for what I had thrown out. But I closed the door on this thought, assuming never to see him again.

A few weeks later, my doorbell rang and there on the porch stood this same man clutching in his hands an exquisite wooden bowl. He thanked me again for the privilege of receiving my tree-trash, and as I stared at the bowl, his purpose in hauling off the dead tree parts became evident: Somehow, this man had transformed my trash into a beautiful treasure.

Handing me the bowl, he explained that he wanted me to have it. We stood on the porch as he spoke of the joy it brought him turning a block of discarded wood into the new creation I now held.

Today, that bowl is proudly displayed in my home, and I often reflect on how my life resembles that fallen walnut tree. Away from the nourishment of its roots, the tree had died. Once dead, it was of no use and discarded as trash. Likewise, apart from God, our life-source, we become spiritually dead and useless to his kingdom, deserving to be cast away from his presence. But gratefully, that is not how God's redeeming love works. Like a master artist who creates a beautiful new bowl from dead wood, God's loving redemption takes us fallen and broken beings, recreates us for his glorious purpose, and breathes new life into us. And dear friend, no one is better at redeeming the old, the worn out, and the broken than our loving Father.

TWO KEY VERSES

Chapters 13 and 14 include some unexpected encouragement to help us walk the Christian path. These relate to us because we, too, live in a world where the same two powerful beasts continue to do battle with God's people. We, too, must remain strong and faithful.

Revelation 13:10

The thirteenth chapter of Revelation portrays a frightful situation, because to the faithful of John's time, captivity and death were real possibilities. Although our faith, most likely, has not landed us in a place of severe danger, we are still surrounded by the powerful evils of the world. The Holy Spirit knew we would need encouragement. So, in Revelation 13:10, John wrote, "This [the prevailing evil] calls for patient endurance and faithfulness on the part of God's people."

"Patient endurance and faithfulness" is a tall order when you are in the middle of a crisis and overwhelmed by hardship on all fronts. Yet, that is exactly what we are told to muster up as we face the storms of life. So, friend, it is important to remember, we serve a BIG God!

- Our Big God formed man from dust and breathed into him life (Gen. 2:7). And our Big God desires to breathe new life into our worn-out and broken existence.

- Our Big God raised the dead (Acts 2:23-24), so when all feels hopeless, he can raise up a new spirit within us.
- Our Big God turned water into wine (John 2:1-11). He can turn our sorrow into joy and our tears into blessings.
- Our Big God healed the sick (John 4:446-53), so we should never doubt his ability to heal whatever heartbreak we are living.

When we find ourselves surrounded by chaos and our fear overwhelms us, remember our big problems are held in the hands of a BIGGER GOD!

Revelation 14:12-13

We have discussed how delightful it must have been for John to receive the peaceful vision of God in heaven with his angels and the redeemed. The angels were proclaiming God. One was bearing the Gospel to all the earth, reminiscent of The Great Commission of Mark 16:15. A second angel was proclaiming God's triumph over evil. And a third was sending out warnings to those siding with the beasts. But following these warnings, we discover another key admonition. Revelation 14:12-13 says:

Here is the patience of the saints; here are those who keep the commandments of God and the faith of Jesus. Then I heard a voice from heaven saying to me, "Write: Blessed are the dead who die in the Lord from now on." "Yes," says the

Spirit, "that they may rest from their labors, and their works follow them."

I love that John's vision is inclusive here of the God-Head. God the Father, God the Son (Jesus Christ), and God the Spirit (the Holy Spirit) all three are represented. Let's consider each one.

God, the Father

The Revelation 14:12 statement refers to, "the commandments of God." According to 2 Timothy 3:16, scripture contains "the commandments of God," the Father. These words were breathed from his very lungs. God's Word teaches us his commands, corrects us when we fail, and guides us in living a righteous life. Today, God's Word continues to serve this same purpose. Dear friend, these commandments of God, our Father, will mold our lives into beautiful vessels.

God, the Son

Next, we find a mention of "the faith of Jesus." While on earth, Jesus, the Son of God and part of the God-Head, demonstrated faith in action. His faith was filled with compassion as he healed and touched the outcasts in society (Matt. 8:1-3). His faithful teachings taught us a new way of loving that placed others ahead of self (Phil. 2:3). Christ's faithful example of humility, mercy, and peace amid trials showed us how to be light in a dark world (Matt. 5:16). Jesus, peacefully asleep during a storm at sea, displayed his absolute faith and trust in the Father (Matt. 8:23-27). And Jesus taking a knee to wash the feet of his disciples taught us all how to become faithful, humble servants (John 13:1-17).

God, the Spirit

Lastly, we have a mention of God's Spirit. Revelation 14:13 records, "Blessed are the dead who die in the Lord from now on. Yes, says the Spirit, that they may rest from their labors, and their works follow them" (Rev. 14:13b). The Holy Spirit, part of the God-Head, is here said to offer us rest from our labors, which is one of the attributes of the Holy Spirit. John 14:26 tells us the Holy Spirit is our comforter; therefore providing us "rest" from our labors falls right within His skill set.

God's People

Now, let's consider our legacy. When Revelation 14:13 says, "Their works follow them," it serves as a reminder that one day our final breath will be taken, and we will transition to a heavenly life with Christ and the redeemed. What we leave behind will be determined by how we have lived while on this earth. We desire our legacy to be written by the actions of our humble hearts and by our praise and admiration of our Holy God. As Christians, we should live in a way that continues to bring souls to God's throne long after our final breath.

LIVING A HOLY LIFE IN PREPARATION OF JUDGEMENT

We have investigated the evils roaming the earth and we are assured that one day all will stand in the presence of our sovereign God and face judgement. So, our desire is to live a holy life and hear that sweet welcome from the Father, "Well done, good and faithful servant" (Matt. 25:23). "Inherit the kingdom prepared for you from the foundation of the world" (Matt. 25:34).

So, what does a holy life resemble? Hebrews 11 offers us inspiration from those who were far from perfect yet lived holy lives through the gift of redemption. Noah, Abraham, and Moses are but a few who fully submitted to God regardless of the cost. Their faith-filled lives have become part of our "Great cloud of witnesses" (Heb. 12:1). From them, we discover courage to "lay aside every weight, and the sin which so easily ensnares us, and let us run with endurance the race that is set before us, looking unto Jesus, the author and finisher of our faith" (Hebrews 12:1-2). Listed below are some ways for us to be victorious in this race of life.

To Live Holy, Follow Christ's Teachings

Mary, the mother of Jesus, offered us poignant advice on what to do with the teachings of Jesus. As she observed an embarrassing predicament for the bridal family when their wine ran out, she gathered the servants, pointed to Jesus, and said, "Whatever He says to you, do it" (John 2:5). Consider the eternal relevance of these words. If we heeded these words and did whatever Jesus said, might our lives and the lives of those around us be drastically and eternally different?

To Live Holy, Discover God's Power Living Within You

In Judges 6 we meet a man named Gideon. What an unfortunate first impression we get of him as we discover him hiding in fear. An angel of the Lord appears and addresses him as "You mighty man of valor" (Judg. 6:12). Obviously, Gideon is confused. These words are far from the man Gideon thinks himself to be. Yet, we discover that this is the man Gideon will become. In Judges 6:14 when God tells Gideon to "Go in this might of yours. . . Have I not sent you?" Gideon discovers thats God's strength already lay within him. Gideon learns if God calls you, God empowers you. Our powerful God does the same for us today. So, friend, God has called you, too. Go discover the strength of the Lord that lies within you and be amazed at the way God will demonstrate his mighty power through your life.

To Live Holy, Forsake Sinful Living and Seek Redemption

No life can be holy apart from God. Second Samuel 11-12 allows us to observe how quickly sin can consume lives and prohibit us from being holy. King David's sin has left him in great need of redemption. After his eyes are opened to his transgressions, we are privileged to walk alongside him as he returns to God. David's journey is recorded in Psalm 51, so we can know how to stand holy before

God after sin has separated us from His Holy presence. Here is the journey:

Admit our sin. David writes in Psalm 51:3, "For I acknowledge my transgressions, and my sin is always before me. Against You, and You only, have I sinned." Yes, our sin, too, is against God, and requires that we admit it and make amends.

Submit our lives to God. In Psalm 51:10 David cries out, "Create in me a clean heart, O God, and renew a steadfast spirit within me." David is aware that redemption lay in God's hand. God alone can renew David's holy life again, but only after David re-submits his life to Holy God.

Commit our lives to God and his people, then move forward. Psalm 51:13 records, "Then, I will teach transgressors Your ways, and sinners will be converted to You." Has it ever dawned on you that as King, sinful David could have hidden his whole sordid affair and murderous act? He could have swept it all under the rug and instituted a "gag order" at the palace to save his reputation. Yet, David chose to make his sinful journey public so we may know the dangers of sin and the beauty of redemption.

CONCLUSION

As we conclude our look at Revelation 13-14, let's consider the words penned by the writer, Jude. Perhaps it was the providence of God that placed the book of Jude just prior to the book of Revelation. Little could Jude have known how his final words would serve as the perfect segway into the book of Revelation and perfectly sum up God's vision to John.

> Now to Him who is able to keep you from stumbling, and to present you faultless before the presence of his glory with exceeding joy, to God our Savior, who alone is wise, be glory and majesty, dominion and power, both now and forever. Amen. (Jude 24)

So dear friend, we will conclude with the very words from which we began.

> *Life can be a battle, but in the end, mighty God wins!*
> *Remain faithful!*

QUESTIONS

1. Check out these scriptures and consider how our lives might become more holy.
   2 Corinthians 7:1
   2 Timothy 1:9
   Romans 12:1

2. Consider the life we might have if we lived in response to the beautiful redemption that Christ offers.

3. What might need to be eliminated or added in our lives so that we may live holy?

4. We must have a humble heart to seek forgiveness. Find scripture references on humility that will help your journey to forgiveness.

 **Rita Cato Cochrane** was born and raised in Nashville, Tennessee where she received her degree in Education from Lipscomb University. Her father, Willie Cato, was a minister of the gospel who worked closely with Marshall Keeble. Her mother was a sought-after ladies Bible class teacher and speaker.

Rita is married to her high school sweetheart, Michael Cochrane, who serves as a shepherd in the church. She is mother to three adult children, grandmother to six rambunctious boys, and "American Mom" to four international students.

Rita taught middle school for twenty-five years. Today, Rita serves as the Director of Women's Ministries at the church of Christ in Green Hills. She also speaks and teaches for conferences, Bible classes, lectureships, and Ladies' Days in the U.S. and abroad. At home in Nashville, Tennessee, Rita teaches ladies Bible classes, hosts a "Women Mentoring Women" Bible study group, and writes a weekly email devotional called "Monday Meditation." She is the author of a women's Bible study book entitled, *Lace Up Those Sneakers, Let's Take a Walk with God*. Her second women's class book was released in the spring of 2023 entitled, *Untying Yesterday's Knots*. She was featured on TBN television show, "The Author's Showcase." Rita also serves on the board of Healing Hands International, a Christian based non-profit that empowers and equips those in need worldwide.

Her hobbies include hiking, walking, cooking for her large family, and traveling the world. (She and husband have traveled to six continents but declare Antarctica too cold to visit).

Because He is Striking His Enemies, I Can Stand for Truth

Revelation 18

Rebecca Young

WHAT IS THE BIG PICTURE?

Throughout the book of Revelation there is an apocalyptic message that challenges our worldview and questions our allegiance. The prevailing thought that questions which side you are standing on is presented over and over in John's message. God is asking us to choose a side, are we with him or are we against him? Of course, as Christians, we will say that we are with him, but there are two positions that we might find ourselves in that challenge our commitment to him. Those times are when we become afflicted or when we become complacent. The pain and sorrow that comes with affliction, challenges our faith, and may cause us to question God and doubt his presence. As humans, we see things from an earthly perspective, and we wonder where God is when we suffer. This can be very perplexing because we want to stop the pain and want to be rescued immediately from our trials. In another instance, we enjoy the luxuries of life and find ourselves drifting into complacency forgetting God and his commands. The world around us is constantly trying to lure us into its lap of luxury. Revelation offers a remedy for both problematic states of faith. God's message to his people, spoken through John, is two-fold providing comfort to the afflicted and a rebuke to the complacent (Stevenson 103). Revelation addresses important contemporary issues on how to stand firmly and faithfully in a world filled with evil and suffering as well as how to stand in allegiance to God by not allowing ourselves to be enticed by the luxuries and conveniences of this world. Will you allow your experiences with suffering or evil things to diminish your faith? Will you chase after the things of this world allowing yourself to forsake your Lord and compromise your obedience to his teachings? Will you stand for truth? These are the big questions Revelation invites its readers to consider. In chapter eighteen, there is an emphasis on complacency, and we will explore how God calls us to stand up and to stand out.

THE FALL OF BABYLON THE GREAT

The "city of Babylon" is used metaphorically in many places throughout the Bible to refer to a wicked and sinful place or people. There was an actual ancient city of Babylon located on the lower

Euphrates River in Mesopotamia, which was at one point in time a massive, powerful, and sprawling city teeming with homes, people, palaces, and temples. Amazingly, in the present state, what was once known as mighty Babylon is now an "extensive field of ruins" in what we today call Iraq (Saggs 2023). Babylon was known as one of the most influential, political, and powerful empires in the world, but today it is a pile of ruins. John uses apocalyptic symbolism to call our attention to recognize how despite the outer appearance of strength, Babylon represents a fallen world, and he uses that symbolism to teach us to remain unscathed from the wrath that will come upon her.

Revelation 17 ends saying, "And the woman whom you saw *is that great city* which reigns over the kings of the earth" (18). [All scripture references are from New King James Version unless otherwise noted]. According to John's message, Babylon reigned over all the governing rulers and authorities of all the earth. In this chapter, there is a dualism between two kingdoms: the kingdom of God, and the kingdom of the earth (Stevenson 98). We are living in the presence of these opposing worlds, and we are being called to make a choice. God is making his appeal to us to recognize that although Babylon appears to be massive, powerful, extravagant, and secure, she is a fallen kingdom filled with sin and evil.

In Revelation 18, an angel cries out, "Babylon the great is fallen, is fallen" (vv. 2). Later, Babylon is depicted as sinful, self-glorifying, luxurious in her living, arrogant, and a deceiver (vv. 5-7, 23). It is important to recognize here that Babylon is being described as *fallen* prior to the wrath of God coming upon her. She is not a fallen city because of God's wrath. She is a fallen city because of her sin, and because of her sin, God's wrath will come upon her! God is warning his people to watch out! Make sure you have not fallen in the same sin as Babylon, so that you will not also be destroyed along with the sinful world. Ask yourself if you have become complacent in your relationship with God to the point of ruin. Because he is striking his enemies, will you stand for truth?

A DWELLING PLACE OF DEMONS, A PRISON, AND A CAGE

This world is not my home, I'm just a-passing through. At times, when we have our eyes fixed on heaven, our home, we can clearly see God's purpose and plan. However, we live in a very distracting world that is constantly pulling our eyes and focus from where it needs to be. If we are not careful, we might find ourselves complacent in this fallen world and devoted to deceitful teachings of demons (1 Tim. 4:1). If we are not careful, the world around us might lull us into not paying attention to our spiritual reality.

Revelation brings the reality of the spiritual realm to the forefront of our minds. We go about our daily lives and do not often think about angels and demons or consider what we may be entertaining could possibly be things *taught by demons*. Living in this physical world as a spiritual being requires us not only to acknowledge the carnal, but also to be aware of the unseen, the spiritual realm. Mature Christian faith does not turn a blind eye to reality, but faces it (Stevenson 44). "For we do not wrestle against flesh and blood, but against principalities, against powers, against the rulers of the darkness of this age, against spiritual hosts of wickedness in the heavenly places" (Eph. 6:12). The angel in Revelation 18:2 is warning that this world has become a dwelling place of demons, a prison for every foul spirit, and a cage for every unclean and hated bird!" The world around us that appears so strong, successful, and mighty is, in reality, a collapsed prison where demons reside.

Is this really a world that a Christian would *want* to be in partnership with? No, but sometimes, we somehow find ourselves trapped and we don't know how we got so entangled. Complacency is not something we knowingly choose; it is something we drift into like a piece of wood drifting out to sea. Before we know it, we are in deep waters and in danger. According to the Cambridge Dictionary, complacency is a feeling of calm satisfaction with your own abilities or situation that prevents you from trying harder. Are you just drifting along in your Christian life, allowing the things of this world to carry you further and further away from God and his truth? Do not allow yourself to be soothed or satisfied by what others in this world are doing to feel good. We are warned by Paul to not conform to the pattern of this world (Rom. 12:2). To conform means to behave according to what is usual or expected by society. Remember, we live in a fallen world and a *dwelling place of demons.*

In Colossians 2:8, Paul again warns the Saints, saying, "Beware lest anyone cheat you through philosophy and empty deceit, according to the tradition of men, according to the basic principles of the world, and not according to Christ." The words *cheat you* here in other versions of the Bible say *plunder you or take you captive.* Don't be deceived into following the basic practices of this world.

We live in a society that embraces materialism as a lifestyle, wealth, and power as the ultimate good, pornography as harmless sexual expression, gambling as a form of revenue and the idolization of celebrity figures as normal (Stevenson 17). "For all the nations have drunk of the wine of the wrath of her fornication, the kings of the earth have committed fornication with her, and the merchants of the earth have become rich through the abundance of her luxury" (Rev. 18:3). The world, with its luxuries and conveniences, is intoxicating, causing many to commit *fornication.* If you are engaged on social media, or any kind of media, you are being enticed on a regular basis to seek after money, material possessions, riches, outward beauty, luxury, power, control, and not only to seek after them, but also to rely on them. Are you drinking the *wine of the wrath of her fornication*? Have you *become rich* through the abundance of her luxury?

Be careful, do not be satisfied by things of this world causing you to compromise your faith. Instead, be satisfied with the things of God. The world and its ways are a trap, a prison, a cage, and a dwelling place of demons! According to the book of Revelation, faithful Christianity does not necessarily lead to a life of comfort and blessing, but to affliction (Stevenson 49). We should not seek after or run after things that will bring us comfort. We need to run after Jesus! Jesus said, "In the world you will have tribulation;

but be of good cheer, I have overcome the world" (John 16:33). Our Christian walk does not guarantee freedom from hardship, pain or suffering, but God will give us the strength to endure hardship, to stand firm in the face of opposition and to come out victorious on the other side. Seek him and flee the chains of complacency and compromise.

COME OUT OF HER, MY PEOPLE!

Before we can stand for truth, we must first decide which side we are standing on. God says, "Be faithful until death, and I will give you the crown of life" (Rev. 2:10b). We are called to be faithful through all, in all, and until all is done. God is striking down his enemies, and if he is striking down his enemies, would you want to be found among those on enemy lines? John says, "He who sins is of the devil, for the devil has sinned from the beginning. For this purpose, the Son of God was manifested, that He might destroy the works of the devil" (1 John 3:8). The English Standard Version of this verse says, "Whoever makes a practice of sinning is of the devil" which is more explanatory stating that people who belong to the devil abide in sin and make a *practice* of it. If we allow sin to abide in us through complacency, we might find ourselves on the wrong side of the battle. John defines evil in the book of Revelation as that which stands in opposition to the kingdom of God (Stevenson 109). This study is asking us to take a deep look at our lives and examine which side we are standing on? Are you standing on the

Lord's side, or are you standing with the world? Look at what James says,

> Adulterers and adulteresses! Do you not know that friendship with the world is enmity with God? Whoever therefore wants to be a friend of the world makes himself an enemy of God. Or do you think that the Scripture says in vain, "The Spirit who dwells in us yearns jealously?" But He gives more grace. Therefore, He says: "God resists the proud, but gives grace to the humble." (Jas. 4:4)

The Greek word used for friendship here refers to having *fondness* of the world, and enmity written in the original language has to do with a strong dislike, hatred, and a reason for opposition. Do we want to be in opposition to God?

In a parable about leaving all to follow him in Luke 14, Jesus used an analogy about two kings at war to teach that if a lesser king is going to war against a greater king, it would be wise for that king to sit down and consider that as the weaker king there will not be victory over the greater king. Knowing that he will lose and be overwhelmed, possibly to the point of death, the weaker king should ask for terms of peace. In wisdom, the weaker king could join forces with the greater and stronger king, even if that meant becoming the other king's servant. Jesus was using these terms of war and peace to teach us how to make peace with God, the greatest King of all! Let us recognize, we are that weaker king and God is the greater king! We cannot fight against God! Not that we would knowingly fight against him, but we do not ever want to find our-selves in a position where he opposes us! Therefore, we must make wise decisions to remain on the side of the greatest King and in his good standing with total compliance! This includes not choosing *fondness* of the world. Jesus concludes the parable saying, "So like-wise, whoever of you does not forsake all that he has cannot be My disciple" (Luke 14:33). We cannot follow Jesus if we are going to stand in opposition to him. Our God is calling us to stand up for truth by standing out from the world!

When we read in Revelation 18:4"And I heard another voice from heaven saying, 'Come out of her, my people,'" God is making an appeal to his precious children (Rev. 18:4). He warns us to come out from among the world and stand with him, "Lest you share in her sins and lest you receive her plagues" (v. 4). Whose side are you living on? God makes it clear, there are two opposing sides, choose one. If you choose the world and share in the sin, then you will be held accountable for your sins and you will face judgment and wrath along with the world. "For her sins have reached to heaven, and God has remembered her iniquities" (Rev. 18:5). The Saints who will not separate themselves will no longer receive pardoning and will partake in judgment. Believers simply cannot have fellowship with a belief system that is fundamentally against what God is all about. God commands us not to have fellowship with lawlessness.

> Do not be unequally yoked together with unbelievers. For what fellowship has righteousness with lawlessness? And what communion has light with darkness? And what accord

has Christ with Belial? Or what part has a believer with an unbeliever? And what agreement has the temple of God have with idols? (2 Cor. 6:14-16)

God is *righteous* and he cannot have anything to do with lawlessness. He is *light* and he cannot have anything to do with darkness. As his daughters, are we in fellowship with him? Are we in agreement with him, or are we sharing a yoke with the world? Think about the yoke and oxen analogy. When you are yoked with anything, you are connected closely and wherever it goes, you will go also. Imagine handcuffing yourself to a thief, a deceiver, or a prostitute. Wherever they go, whatever they do, you are there with them. This sounds absurd! *This* is what God is trying to show us and warn us about. He is desperately warning us to come out from *Babylon*. See clearly, with spiritual eyes, how absurd it is to yoke ourselves with a sinful world. He wants us to come to a sober realization about our choices as he cries desperately, "Come out of her, my people, lest you share in her sins, and lest you receive of her plagues" (Rev. 18:4). He wants us to stand with him in truth, so that he can protect us because *he will* strike his enemies.

GOD, OUR FATHER, OUR PROVIDER

This world we live in encourages us to rely on things that give us a false sense of security. It promotes reliance on material possessions, money, power and most of all, self. Self-reliance, in the Cambridge

Dictionary, is defined as the quality of not needing help or support from other people. This social construct of self-reliance opposes the teachings of God. He created us not to be alone (Gen. 2:18). He created us for community, family, and fellowship (John 13:34; 1 Cor. 1:10; Gal. 6:2; Matt. 18:20). He wants to be our father and our provider of all things (Matt. 6; Phil. 4:19). If we fail to rely on God, our father, we hinder our fellowship with him. More importantly, we subtly join in with the world becoming complacent and self-reliant. Remember the characteristics of Babylon. "In the measure that she glorified herself and lived luxuriously, in the same measure give her torment and sorrow; for she says in her heart, 'I sit as queen, and am no widow, and will not see sorrow'" (Rev. 18:7). There is a false sense of security in luxurious living and deception in self-reliance. In the very next verse, God says that plagues, along with death, mourning, and famine will come her way because Babylon will soon face the judgment and wrath of the living God. God is giving us a wakeup call so that we can choose wisely and partake of his love instead of his wrath.

God is the provider of all things. He wants to live in us and wants us to live in him. After commanding us not to be yoked with unbelievers Paul writes,

> For you are the temple of the living God. As God has said: "I will dwell in them and walk among them. I will be their God, and they shall be My people." Therefore "Come out from among them and be separate, says the Lord. Do not touch what is unclean, and I will receive you." "I will be a

Father to you, and you shall be My sons and daughters, says the Lord Almighty." (2 Cor. 6:16-18)

God wants to be our provider, our father. He wants to take care of us and yoke himself to us. The Lord Almighty, Lord of Lords, King of Kings, wants to live in us and make us his own. First Peter 2:9-10 says that we are "His own special people," and he made us his own so that we may be called "out of darkness" and brought "into His marvelous light." Our father wants to provide a secure dwelling place for us that is marvelous! This world has nothing to offer, and God has everything to offer. Will you stand with your God and take *his* yoke upon you instead?

LAMENTING WITH THE KINGS AND MERCHANTS

What moves your soul? Do you weep and mourn over things that the world weeps and mourns over? If society as we know it was destroyed, would you be sad? In Revelation 18, we see that the kings of the earth and the merchants of the earth "weep and mourn" over the destruction of Babylon. The voice from heaven says, "'The kings of the earth who committed fornication and lived luxuriously with her will weep and lament for her, when they see the smoke of her burning, standing at a distance for fear of her torment, saying, 'Alas, alas, that great city Babylon, that mighty city! For in one hour your judgment has come'" (Rev. 18:9-10). The kings of the earth were weeping and lamenting because their mighty city in which they put all their trust and reliance was swiftly coming down to ruin. Later, we see the merchants weep and mourn because they are no longer able to get rich and everything that they saw as a splendid resource has come to nothing (Rev. 18:11;16-17). If society as you know it would come to nothing before your eyes, would you weep and mourn over it? What if you lost your job, your home, your material possessions, would you be devastated, not sad, devastated? What if your hometown was destroyed, would you be crushed, not hurt, crushed? Where do you place your hope? The kings and merchants placed their hope in riches, power, and false strength. When Babylon was destroyed, they were devastated. Our true values are often demonstrated in times of pressure or duress. Our core beliefs and values are seen in what we grieve.

What the kings and merchants fail to see is that the Almighty God is striking down his enemies. Why can't they see God and what he is doing? It is because their hearts and minds are in the wrong place. They unknowingly are not standing on the right side. They lament over wrong things and for the wrong reasons. Are you lamenting with the kings and merchants of this world? God wants us to stand with him. If we have fallen into complacency and have allowed ourselves to be yoked with this world, we might also find ourselves on the wrong side of things lamenting with the kings and merchants. For the Christian, lament should grow out of an acknowledgement that the world is not as it ought to be (Stevenson 44). This is the proper Christian response! Christians who accept loss as God's sovereignty and providence have their mind in the right place. We know that we can trust our Heavenly Father and he will work all things out for our good (Rom. 8:28). Because God is striking his enemies, I can stand on the side of truth!

FEAR NOT! BEHOLD, YOUR GOD!

For the compromised and comfortable Christian, the purpose of John's message is to provide a call to action, to wake up! Recognize the illusion of security and prosperity that the king of this world tries to tempt you with wealth and self-reliance. Open your eyes to the reality that God is on his throne, he opposes all things that set themselves up against him, and he *will* destroy all that is evil. We must be on the right side of this! Revelation makes it clear that there is no dual citizenship in *Babylon*, nor *New Jerusalem*. We must choose a side! One must align oneself with the kingdom of God or the kingdom of this world (Stevenson 101). Wake up and choose God! In choosing God and his kingdom we will have nothing to fear. Isaiah 35:4 says, "Say to those who are fearful-hearted, 'Be strong, do not fear! Behold, your God will come with vengeance, with the recompense of God; He will come and save you." God's vengeance will come. His judgment will come. His wrath will come. Those of us who are standing on the side of truth will be safe and secure. Psalm 91:1-2 says, "He who dwells in the secret place of the Most High shall abide under the shadow of the Almighty. I will say of the Lord, 'He is my refuge and my fortress; My God, in Him I will trust." A mighty fortress and shelter is our

God! He is our refuge (Ps. 46:1). He will do anything to protect us from evil, even personal sacrifice. We find solace in knowing that the very reason God sent his one and only son to the earth was to destroy the works of the evil one and to save us (1 John 3:8; John 12:47). Jesus is the greatest example of how to embrace the Father's will and how to seek to glorify him in our earthly bodies.

> Now My soul is troubled, and what shall I say? "Father, save Me from this hour?" But for this purpose, I came to this hour. Father, glorify Your name. Then a voice came from heaven, saying, "I have both glorified it and will glorify it again." Therefore, the people who stood by and heard it said that it had thundered. Others said, "An angel has spoken to Him." Jesus answered and said, "This voice did not come because of Me, but for your sake. Now is the judgment of this world; now the ruler of this world will be cast out." (John 12:27-31)

The day that Jesus died on that cross, the ruler of this world was crushed! God was glorified, his righteousness upheld, and all wickedness was avenged. Jesus encourages us to be of good cheer because he has overcome the world (John 16:33).

CONCLUSION

God's desire for the reader of Revelation is to understand their place within the larger context of life. This book reveals a God who counsels the faithful to stand up to what is evil (Stevenson 47). In

Revelation 18, God is warning us to not be complacent, to be a people who are called out, and to recognize his stance when it comes to wickedness. He opposes all evil and he plans on destroying anything and everything that opposes him. With this knowledge, he wants you to evaluate your current state of faith. Are you standing on the right side of God's truth? Will you compromise your beliefs and join in with the world? We must allow God's revelation to transform our thinking and motivate us to align ourselves with his plan and his will. Because he is striking his enemies, will you stand for truth?

QUESTIONS

1. Do you find yourself complacent in your relationship with God? Are you standing for truth by sharing your faith with those who have not obeyed the gospel?

2. Are you living out Christianity, or are you living out the culture you were brought up in?

3. Have you ever found yourself entangled in a sin and wondered, how did I get here? Share a time that you strayed from God's word and how you were able to get back on track.

4. Name something in society that has a false sense of strength and security but is not in line with God's teachings. Do you think one day it could possibly collapse and be no more? Why do you think this?

5. Identify something in your life that might be giving you a false sense of security. Does this thing bring you more joy than spending time with God?

6. Do you struggle with having a friendship with the world? Do you use your "friendship" with the world to bring souls to Christ? Or do people in the world tend to influence you more than you influence them? What steps can you take to change this?

7. Do you believe that your life is aligned with God right now? If yes, how so? If not, what do you have to change to be more aligned with his will?

BIBLIOGRAPHY

Blue Letter Bible, www.blueletterbible.org. Accessed 13 Sep. 2023.

Cambridge English Dictionary: Definitions & Meanings, <http://dictionary.cambridge.org/us/dictionary/english/>. Accessed 12 Sept. 2023.

Saggs, Henry W.F.. "Babylon". Encyclopedia Britannica, 3 July. 2023, <https://www.britannica.com/place/Babylon-ancient-city-Mesopotamia-Asia>. Accessed 6 September 2023.

Stevenson, Gregory. *A Slaughtered Lamb: Revelation and the Apocalyptic Response to Evil and Suffering*. Abilene Christian UP, 2013.

 **Rebecca Young** joined Christ in baptism 31 years ago in April 1992, and immediately became an active member of the Stony Brook University Campus Ministry. One of her first invitees to church was Rob Young, the man who would later become her husband, and who is now an elder of the Long Island Church of Christ. Within her first three years in Christ, Rebecca was blessed to be used by God to bring her parents and three siblings to join her in the Kingdom. Her father, Steve Aponte Sr., is also an elder in the Long Island Church of Christ, and her two brothers serve as deacons there as well.

Rob and Rebecca have three children, Leah, Hannah, and Robert Jr. who were all homeschooled by Rebecca and have attended or are recent graduates of Freed-Hardeman University. All their children are also active members of the Lord's Church.

Rebecca loves teaching women the Bible, cooking, baking and being hospitable, and she enjoys having a house full of people that she can share her food and fellowship with. Her favorite passage of scriptures are Psalm 46:10 and Proverbs 3:5-6. Rebecca is a devoted wife, mother, and follower of Jesus. She does her best to live for God first, love her husband and children, and serve her family in Christ.

Because He is Arranging a Banquet, I Can Feast on His Word

Revelation 19:7-10

Kathy Pollard

To fully appreciate this study, we must start with an understanding of ancient weddings. Most of the time young people did not get to choose whom they would marry. That decision was arranged by their parents. However, there were some marriages of love or a young man could make his preference known. Remember how Jacob fell in love with Rachel and was willing to work for her hand in marriage (Gen. 29:18-20)? [All scripture references are from the English Standard Version unless otherwise noted.] And Song of Solomon certainly depicts love and romance between a married couple.

For the wedding itself, the bridegroom would dress in fine garments and wear some sort of crown. He would then make his way to the bride's house. It must have looked like a parade as he was accompanied by his friends who were playing musical instruments. Meanwhile the bride had much preparation to make. She needed to be purified and cleansed, dressed in finery, and adorned with jewels. She would also have been completely covered with a veil. Imagine how she must have felt as she awaited the bridegroom's arrival! When the groom showed up, he would then escort his veiled bride back to his house. They would be accompanied by friends and family who were playing instruments and dancing and singing songs to the couple. Did you know that Psalm 45 is a love song that was sung at royal weddings? No wonder the opening words are, "My heart overflows with a pleasing theme" (Ps. 45:1). Imagine singing to the wedding couple,

"All glorious is the princess in her chamber,
with robes interwoven with gold.
In many-colored robes she is led to the king,
with her virgin companions following behind her.
With joy and gladness they are led along
as they enter the palace of the king" (v. 13-15).

Joy and gladness! Weddings have been an occasion for celebration for millennia. The guests would enjoy a big multi-day feast and the bridegroom would present gifts to his bride. For more information about ancient weddings, visit bible-history.com or consult Zondervan's *Archaeological Study Bible*.

The text for our study is Revelation 19:7-10. When John recorded this wedding announcement, it was the crescendo to the promise of victory in the previous chapter. It was heralded by "a great multitude, like the roar of many waters and like the sound of mighty peals of thunder, crying out, 'Hallelujah!…the marriage of the Lamb has come…'" (vv. 6,7). This wedding proclamation would have surely evoked an emotional response from the hearers, one of promise, hope, commitment, and celebration. With a great multitude shouting the happy news, it was sure to be the wedding party to end all wedding parties!

From this marriage vision near the end of inspiration, we learn more about our God. He stands up for us, protects us, and wants to bless us. This confirms what he has been showing us all along in his Word. Let's take a closer look and see why this wedding invitation is still a reason to celebrate.

THE INVITATION

"And the angel said to me, 'Write this: Blessed are those who are invited to the marriage supper of the Lamb'" (Rev. 19:9). The invitation has been extended. What makes it so special?

It is From the Lamb

The Lamb is Jesus Christ and the bride is His church (2 Cor. 11:2; Rom. 7:4). Why is Jesus called a Lamb? It is because he became our sacrificial lamb (Isa. 53:7; John 1:29; Rev. 12:10,11). When John was given the revelation, he had no doubt who the Lamb was. In the book itself, "Lamb" is mentioned 29 times. Notice what we learn about the Lamb from these references. He is worshiped (5:8; 22:3). He is worthy of power, wealth, wisdom, might, honor, glory, and blessing (5:12). Salvation belongs to him (7:10). He is in the midst of the throne (7:17; 22:1). He is the guiding shepherd (7:17). He is a conqueror (12:11; 17:14). The book of life belongs to him (13:8; 21:27). He is "Lord of lords and King of kings" (17:14). This is who extended the invitation!

Jesus is a groom who chose his own bride out of great love for her. Now that we have more insight into ancient weddings, read the following text with that in mind and underline what the groom (Christ) did and does for his bride (the church).

Husbands, love your wives, as Christ loved the church and gave himself up for her, that he might sanctify her, having cleansed her by the washing of water with the word, so that he might present the church to himself in splendor, without spot or wrinkle or any such thing, that she might be holy and without blemish. In the same way husbands should love their wives as their own bodies. He who loves his wife loves himself. For no one ever hated his own flesh, but nourishes and cherishes it, just as Christ does the church, because we are members of his body. "Therefore a man shall leave his father and mother and hold fast to his wife, and the two shall become one flesh." This mystery is profound, and I am saying that it refers to Christ and the church. (Eph. 5:25-32)

It is to the Marriage Supper

According to the Archaeological Study Bible, a Jewish marriage feast would have lasted for seven days and would have been hosted by the groom's family (1039). Much care and preparation would have been put into such an event. The very best food and drink would have been offered. It was an honor to be invited!

Perhaps John harkened back to Jesus' parable of the wedding feast. "A king gave a wedding feast for his son, and sent his servants to call those who were invited to the wedding feast, but they would not come" (Matt. 22:2-3). He sent more servants out to explain that everything was ready. He "prepared the dinner" and "slaughtered the fat calves." Special preparations had been made at his own personal expense, but "they paid no attention" (vv. 4-5). This parable would have created quite a stir. Who would do such a thing? Who would reject an invitation to a king's marriage feast? In Revelation, John heard an invitation "to the marriage supper of the Lamb," the King of kings!

THE RESPONSE

In Jesus' parable of the wedding supper, the invitees ignored the invitation and went about their business. Some even reacted angrily to those who conveyed the invitation. But on the occasion that John saw, the response was completely different.

Rejoicing and Exulting

The great multitude shouted, "Let us rejoice and exult!" (Rev. 19:7). Remember, this was a celebration of victory. Revelation 19 is a chapter filled with hallelujahs and praises because of what God would do to Rome on behalf of his people. "Hallelujah! Salvation and glory and power belong to our God, for his judgments are true and just...he has avenged the blood of his servants" (v. 2). "Hallelujah! For the Lord our God the Almighty reigns" (v. 6).

Giving Glory and Worshiping

The great multitude continued, "give him the glory, for the marriage of the Lamb has come" (Rev. 19:7). After John heard the shouts of the multitude, the angel said to him, "Blessed are those who are invited to the marriage supper of the Lamb." The angel went on to give a seal of assurance by adding, "These are the true words of God" (v. 9). When John heard that, "he fell down at his feet to worship him." The angel explained that he was not to be worshipped and told John, "Worship God" (v. 10). Most references to the Lamb in Revelation involve worship.

The response was one of celebration. It was one of rejoicing and exultation. It involved giving God glory and worship. We rejoice also! We are not persecuted by Rome, but we look forward to the coming of the groom. Jesus will escort us back to his eternal home where we will be under his protection forever.

For the Lord himself will descend from heaven with a cry of command, with the voice of an archangel, and with the sound of the trumpet of God. And the dead in Christ will rise first. Then we who are alive, who are left, will be caught up together with them in the clouds to meet the Lord in the air, and so we will always be with the Lord. Therefore encourage one another with these words. (1 Thess. 4:16-18)

Recently a young lady in our church family got married. A couple of weeks later another young lady got married. Do you know what was obvious about both of those women? They were excited about their wedding days. For months they have been grinning and planning and laughing. Every time someone brought up the subject of their upcoming marriages, their eyes lit up. Both of those women were happily in love and could not wait to spend a lifetime with their future husbands. They were filled with anticipation and everyone knew it!

Faithful Christians have much to anticipate. We already have a relationship with our Lord, and it should be obvious to everyone that we look forward to spending an eternity with him. A great day of celebration is coming! Are you excited? Can others tell? Do you smile and want to talk about it and plan for it?

GETTING READY

"The marriage of the Lamb has come, and his Bride has made herself ready" (Rev. 19:7).

Purification

As we already mentioned, the bride would purify herself in preparation for the coming of her bridegroom. How did the Lamb's bride make herself ready? She washed herself in his blood (Rev. 7:14). There is significance in the blood of the Lamb:

- We are justified by his blood (Rom. 5:9).
- It cleanses us from all sin (1 John 1:7; Matt. 26:28).
- It washes away our sins (Rom. 1:5; Rev. 1:5-6).
- It redeems us (Heb. 9:12).
- It purges the conscience (Heb. 9:14).
- It sanctifies us (Heb. 13:12).
- By it our sins are forgiven (Col. 1:14).
- It is our propitiation (Rom. 3:25).
- It gives us boldness to enter the presence of God (Heb. 10:19).
- It purchased the church/ bride (Acts 20:28).
- And it brings near those who were afar off (Eph. 2:13).

How does one contact that precious blood? The answer is found within the divine connection between the blood and baptism. Jesus shed his blood when he died on the cross (John 19:34), and we are baptized into his death (Rom. 6:3). His blood was shed for the remission of sins (Matt. 26:28), and baptism is for the remission of sins (Acts 2:38). His blood washed us from our sins (Rev. 1:5), and baptism washes away our sins (Acts 22:16). His blood sanctifies us (Heb. 13:12), and the washing of water sanctifies the bride of Christ (Eph. 5:25-27).

That is how the bride of Christ makes herself ready. She is purified by his blood which she contacts through baptism. The bride is the church which is made up of all those who have put on Christ in baptism (Gal. 3:27). Are you a part of the bride of Christ? Have you made yourself ready to meet the Lamb?

The Dress

"And to her it was granted to be arrayed in fine linen, clean and bright, for the fine linen is the righteous acts of the saints" (Rev. 19:8). The use of linen is found many times in the Bible. It was often made of flax and used for garments, rope, thread, napkins, turbans, and lamp wicks. "Fine linen" probably referred to an Egyptian linen that was particularly white and soft. It was valuable and costly. It is what Pharoah robed Joseph in (Gen. 41:42) and what King David wore when he celebrated the return of the ark (1 Chron. 15:25-28). It is what the "virtuous woman" wore and why she sought flax (Prov. 31:22). And it is what the angels are clothed in (Rev. 15:6) and the armies in Heaven wear (Rev. 19:11-14). Fine linen was symbolic of purity...purity of the angels and purity of the bride of Christ. It is a symbol of moral purity, "clean and bright."

The fine linen the bride wears is "the righteous acts of the saints." According to the Bible, all Christians are saints (see Acts 9:13, 32; 26:10; Phil. 4:21). This makes sense since we have already seen that the Bride of the Lamb is the church.

What are the "righteous acts?" We see the term used earlier in the book. "Who will not fear, O Lord, and glorify your name? For you alone are holy. All nations will come and worship you, for your righteous acts have been revealed" (Rev. 15:4). We can also find it in other New Testament passages. In Romans 1:32, it is God's "righteous decree." In Romans 2:26, it is "precepts" (or "requirements"). In Romans 8:4, it is the "righteous requirement" of the law. And in Hebrews 9:1, it refers to the "regulations" of a covenant. It is more than just moral living. It is being made right with God. We are starting to get a sense of the significance of the deeds the bride is clothed in. Her gown is fine linen, clean and bright, because she fulfills the commandments of God. She has made herself right with God.

Standing Out

When you see a wedding party, you do not have to wonder which woman is the bride. She is easily recognized by her very dress. In the same way, we should be recognizable by our dress, our fine linen, our righteous acts. The world should not have to wonder whether or not we belong to Christ.

Can you imagine going to a wedding where the bride tries to hide herself or camouflage her appearance? What if she refused to wear the white gown because she did not want anyone to know that she was the one getting married? We would think there was something wrong. She would look just like the rest of the guests. The guests would be surprised and say, "You're the bride?" But sometimes the bride of Christ does not stand out like she should. It is all too easy for us to blend in with the world, to look and act just like our neighbors or co-workers. Then, if they happen to find out that we are Christians, they are surprised. May a neighbor never look at us and say in disbelief, "You're a Christian?" Paul wrote of a "manner worthy of the saints" (Rom. 16:2) and that manner should identify us as the bride of the Lamb.

One of the seven churches of Asia that Revelation was written to was the church at Ephesus. When Paul wrote the epistle to them, he described their "work of ministry" (Eph. 4:12) and encouraged them to be pure. Concerning sexual immorality, unwholesome talk, or greed, Paul said it "must not be named among you, as is proper among saints" (Eph. 5:3). Consider what this would have meant for Christians in Ephesus in the first century. Ephesus was a very prosperous and pagan culture. It was under Roman rule. My husband and I just returned from a Mediterranean Bible tour. While visiting Ephesus, we were impressed by the size of the amphitheater and terraced houses. We walked along the agora (the long market street which would have been lined with shops). We also learned how difficult it was for Christians.

Artemis was the major goddess worshipped in Ephesus. According to Greek mythology, she was the daughter of Zeus. Nearly every aspect of Ephesian living was centered around Artemis. For example, there were at least two major holidays in her honor every year that would have been grand scale festivals. Would Christians participate like everyone else? Artemis was often referred to as "Savior" and "Lady" (the female version of 'Lord'). Women prayed to her for fertility and healthy childbearing. Her temple was one of the seven wonders of the ancient world for its sheer size. It was four times the size of the Parthenon in Athens! It had 127 columns that stood over 60 feet high. "It functioned at the center of the city's economic life" (Beers 17).

While in Ephesus, we learned that there were trade guilds that people needed to be a part of in order to sell their wares. For instance, there were fishmonger guilds that made it easier for one to set up shop on the agora and sell their fish. Many of these guilds would adopt Artemis as their patron. So when it came time for these guilds to meet, it would involve the worship of their "deity." Faithful Christians, of course, would have nothing to do with that, and, therefore, their very livelihood would suffer. Some would try to entice them to compromise by suggesting it was no big deal. After all, they needed to provide for their family, right? Just go ahead and join the guild "in name only" so you could put food on your table! You can see how enticing this would be. According the the Archaeological Study Bible, some scholars believe this is what was being referred to in Revelation 13 (2067). "He also forced everyone, small and great, rich and poor, free and slave, to receive a mark on his right hand or on his forehead, so that no one could buy or sell unless he had the mark, which is the name of the beast or the number of his name (v. 16-17). No wonder Paul admonished them, "Do not become partners with them; for at one time you were darkness, but now you are light in the Lord. Walk as children of light (for the fruit of the light is found in all that is good and right and true), and try to discern what is pleasing to the Lord. Take no part in the unfruitful works of darkness..." (Eph. 5:7-11). It was a true test of faith for Christians to trust that God would provide for their families if they refused to have anything to do with the worship of Artemis or Roman emperors. Or to at least believe that the persecution they would endure for standing against an entire culture would be "nothing compared to the glory to come" (Rom. 8:18).

The Christians under Roman persecution must have felt so marginalized, small, insignificant, helpless. To learn that their faithfulness would be rewarded with victory (Rev. 2:10) and that Rome would be defeated (Rev. 18) would be much needed motivation. But then also to hear of the Lamb coming to claim his bride would have restored their sense of worth and belonging! Indeed, "Blessed are those who are invited to the marriage supper of the Lamb."

QUESTIONS

1. Read Matthew 22:1-14. It was customary for wedding hosts to provide garments for their guests to wear. In what way did one guest stand out, and what did the king ask him? What does this guest's actions say about him? Why was the king angry?

2. In Revelation 19:7-10, there are several words that describe our identity in Christ. See if you can find them.

3. In chapters 2 and 3 of Revelation, the seven churches are addressed. They are commended and rebuked for various things. Compile a list of these things to do or not do to get a picture of how the bride of Christ should look if she is going to stand out today.

4. Think about what it would have been like to live under Roman rule. You would have suffered for believing in only one God or refusing to worship a false god or emperor. You would have been persecuted perhaps to the point of starvation. You may have lost loved ones just for admitting to be a follower of Jesus. Now read Revelation 18:21-24. "Babylon" represented Rome. How would hearing all of those "no more" promises make you feel? Is there a sense in which we should have that same kind of relief and gratitude today? If so, why? And how should it affect our daily walk?

BIBLIOGRAPHY

Beers, Holly. *A Week in the Life of a Greco-Roman Woman*. Downers Grove: InterVarsity, 2019.

Kaiser, Walter C. and Duane Garrett, ed. *NIV Archaeological Study Bible: An Illustrated Walk Through Biblical History and Culture*. Grand Rapids: Zondervan, 2005.

"Marriage in Biblical Times." Ancient Marriage, Bible History: Maps, Images, Archaeology, nd. 1 Nov. 2023. <https://bible-history.com/biblestudy/marriage>.

Kathy Pollard is married to Neal Pollard, who preaches for the Lehman Avenue Church of Christ in Bowling Green, Kentucky. They have three grown sons, all married, and two new grandsons with another grandchild on the way! Kathy attended Faulkner University and Bear Valley Bible Institute and has a bachelor's degree in Bible.

She is the author of the book, *Return to Me…What to Do When Loved Ones Fall Away*. She and Carla Moore host a weekly podcast for Christian women called *Looking Up*. Kathy enjoys spending time with family, traveling to Israel, tending her gardens, and getting to know her new dairy cow, Peaches.

Because He is Preparing a Place, I Will Set My Sight on Heaven

Revelation 21

Cayron J. Mann

INTRODUCTION

After John was instructed to write the letters to the seven churches in Revelation 1-3, after the proclamations of the worthiness of the Lamb in Revelation 6, and after the terrifying woes of great judgment in Revelation 20, John is shown the *new* heaven and the *new* earth. It is of importance to note that John is not just seeing the "next" heaven and earth, nor is it simply a "better" heaven and earth. The Greek word *kaine* is used in the context of Revelation 21:1 meaning "fresh" (enduringword.-com). An entirely *new* heaven and earth, unlike anything that could have been imagined is before John, and now, he has been given the duty of writing so that others will read his testimony of God's immediate actions that "Behold, I am making all things new" (Revelation 21:5) [All scripture references are from the English Standard Version unless otherwise noted].

Even though John probably never dreamed of being given this responsibility, he may have had some ideas about what to expect. After all, he had grown up being taught the prophecies of Isaiah, "For behold, I create new heavens and a new earth, and the former things shall not be remembered or come into mind" (Isa. 65:17). And, no doubt he had often sung the Psalm that contains the lyrics, "Of old you laid the foundation of the earth, and the heavens are the work of your hands. They will perish, but you will remain; they will all wear out like a garment. You will change them like a robe, and they will pass away, but you are the same, and your years have no end" (Ps. 102:25-27).

Even the journey itself must have taken John's breath away! Revelation 21:10 describes one of the seven angels carrying John away "in the Spirit to a great, high mountain" to view "the holy city Jerusalem coming down out of heaven from God, having the glory of God, its radiance like a most rare jewel, like a jasper, clear as crystal." The best John could describe the glow of this city was to compare it to the brilliance of a multicolored jasper stone, perhaps like the ones he had grown up seeing on the breastplates worn by high priests.

The idea of a new heaven and a new earth was not… *new.* But now, John was actually *seeing* it with human eyes and making his very best attempt at describing this eternal and spiritual city

Remember: my citizenship is in Heaven!

with physical words just so we can have a glimpse into the glory that lay before him. It wasn't an easy task, but once John was told to "Write what you see..." (Rev. 1:11), his descriptions in these 27 verses assure us of the careful preparation that is going into this eternal holy city where we will live forever with God.

Onward to the prize before us!

Soon His beauty we'll behold;

Soon the pearly gates will open;

We shall tread the streets of gold.

(Lister)

John, in his awe, could not stop staring at everything the angel was showing him. It's easy to imagine his eyelids widening and blinking, mouth agape, shoulders dropped, perhaps his head was even tilting to one side, and he was having to catch his breath after the supernatural transportation he had just experienced. He may have had to shield his eyes from the brilliance and splendor of the city. And even then, the angel had to keep John on task and nudge him to remind him to "Write this down, for these words are trustworthy and true" (v. 5).

In verse 10 of Revelation 21, the angel is showing John the "holy city Jerusalem coming down out of heaven from God," and he writes descriptions of the colors of the jewels, the gates, and the foundations of the walls of the city. He is shown the massive dimensions of the foursquare city, and he specifically names each and every gemstone that graces the wall of the city. John also describes the unique light which illuminates the city. John Clements, in his beautiful fourth stanza of "No Night There" wrote, "There they need no sunshine bright, In that city four-square; For the Lamb is all the light, And there is no night there."

John closes the chapter with a reminder that "only those who are written in the Lamb's book of life" will enter this holy eternal city (Rev. 21:27). So, in this study, let's pause and consider three simple yet powerful reasons for setting our sights on heaven:

- Because heaven is being prepared for us,
- Because of what will NOT be present,
- Because we have been told what preparations we should be making.

LET US SET OUR SIGHTS ON HEAVEN BECAUSE IT IS BEING PREPARED FOR US

Jesus tells us in John 14:1-2: "Let not your hearts be troubled. Believe in God: believe also in me. In my Father's house are many rooms. If it were not so, would I have told you that I go to prepare a place for you?" Jesus wants us to trust that if he tells us what he is doing, we can take him at his word. "And if I go and prepare a place for you, I will come again and will take you to myself, that where I am you may be also" (John 14:3).

Imagine what our Father's house will be like and to know that there will be a place specifically and intentionally prepared for you. You will be welcomed. You will be in God's presence. You will be home where there will truly be peace, perfect peace. Scripture translations vary from describing heaven as having many mansions or many rooms. But it will be far better than what we think of as earthly mansions. This place that is being prepared will be where we will see God face to face. We will share in his glory, and it will be everlasting. We will no longer be yearning for that day. That day will have come, and eternity will be our reality.

This new heaven and new earth is where our faith and allegiance truly lie. Paul assured the Philippians, "But our citizenship is in heaven, and from it we await a Savior, the Lord Jesus Christ" (Phil. 3:20). And, what God has done away with (the former things) will have no place in what has been made new. Those comforting words of Revelation 21:4 guarantee us of God's comfort and our long-awaited, face-to-face companionship with him. The face-to-face relationship that Adam shared with God in the garden of Eden will finally return, and God will, once again, be among his people (Spurgeon). God will be there! He will be right there among us! And he will be with those we love because we will be together for eternity!

LET US SET OUR SIGHTS ON HEAVEN BECAUSE OF WHAT WILL *NOT* BE THERE

You read that right. It's truly impossible to imagine all that heaven has in store for the saints. When you were a child, you thought as a child, and you may have wondered about whether there would be toys in heaven or whether your favorite pet would be there. Yet, as you became an adult and began to think like an adult, you realized that "the things that I love, and hold dear to my heart are just borrowed, they're not mine at all" (Rambo). We will not want for anything in heaven for God will supply us with every spiritual need imaginable. And yet, there will be an immediate and noticeable absence of some things that many experience daily here in the physical earthly world.

You who are reading this have probably either mourned the loss of a special person or you have ministered to someone who is grieving (or both). Grief is difficult to describe and extremely heavy to navigate. As a professional counselor, I often sit and hold space with those who are experiencing the indescribable pain of loss after the death of a special person. Questions are often asked, like "How long am I going to feel this way?" and "How long does grief last?" It only takes a quick internet search for these questions, and you might find answers like "Six months to two years," and "Most grief symptoms lessen with time." However, the best answer is, "Grief lasts as long as it lasts." In other words, grief is unique for every single person. No one has ever experienced the exact loss that you experienced, because no one experienced the same relationship that you had with the person who died.

Of all the descriptions of heaven in Revelation 21, this 4th verse—"He will wipe away every tear from their eyes, and death shall be no more, neither shall there be mourning, nor crying, nor pain anymore, for the former things have passed away"—describes the powerful action that will occur the very instant we enter heaven. Yes, the structure and the dimensions and the size of heaven are magnificently described. Yet, this vision of John seeing God's eternal compassion greeting saints by wiping away their tears forever is one that stays with us. It will be the absolute end of all of these former things, and the absolute beginning of a place with no cause for any of those things because there will be no death, no mourning, no crying, no pain.

We long for that day, don't we–that day of "no more crying and no more pain." W. Hardman's commentary describes that "the balmy air and the sunny slopes of the new paradise of God will never know anything of the sin, the injustice, and the cruelty, which, by their shadows, darken the heart even of the Christian here. And Bart Millard, in his song, "I Can Only Imagine" expresses as much as our human heart can envision with his lyrics,

I can only imagine / What it will be like

When I walk by Your side / I can only imagine

What my eyes would see / When Your face is before me

I can only imagine / I can only imagine

When that day comes

And I find myself / Standing in the Son

I can only imagine / When all I will do

Is forever, forever worship You

I can only imagine, yeah

I can only imagine.

LET US SET OUR SIGHTS ON HEAVEN BECAUSE WE HAVE BEEN TOLD HOW TO PREPARE

Growing up, I was jealous of my older brothers and all the amazing trips they were always going on with the youth group at church. I couldn't wait until the time that I'd be a "youth!" Every time they would get on that white church bus with blue letters, I had to watch them ride off to singings, fast food restaurants, retreats, scavenger hunts, progressive dinners, and other exciting youth activities. It felt like forever before my turn would come. One Sunday, there was an announcement that the *little* youth were going on a bus trip to the Memphis Zoo. We were to bring a sack lunch and money for snacks and the best part? You guessed it! My brothers didn't get to go. This event was for little kids only!

That very next Saturday morning, my dad drove me to the church building for the big trip. I had prepared all week! And, I had assured my parents over and over that I was ready for this solo trip on the big church bus. Clutching a brown paper lunch bag in hand and a few dollars neatly folded in a ziploc bag, I hopped up onto the bus, ready for a full day's adventure! Odd that this bus seemed much bigger inside than it appears from the outside. I found a seat and eagerly waved to my dad, who was smiling and leaning on his old Ford Falcon, watching for the departure. Here it was, the moment I'd dreamed of! I was leaving on an adventure, all by myself! It was then that I began looking at the size of the bus and thinking about the distance we'd be traveling and that it would be for the entire day, and...it didn't take long to begin seriously reconsidering my life choices. What was I thinking? I'm not old enough to do this! I'm just a kid! I was not nearly as prepared as I thought I was! As you rightfully guessed, my joy quickly turned into fear, and without giving any further thought, I bounded down the bus steps and, with tears flowing, sprinted to my dad's arms. But before I could tell him through my tears that I'd changed my mind about the trip and I couldn't bear the thought of traveling alone, he reached behind the seat of the car, and brought out a paper sack… with a lunch inside it. He asked if I would reconsider going on the trip if he came along with me. I couldn't believe it! The dread left as quickly as it had appeared! There was nothing to fear now that my dad was going! And he had even packed a lunch (which had been stressed as being an important factor in the success of the day). It was the best day ever, complete with souvenirs and unforgettable memories!

A few years later, I can remember asking my dad how he knew that I would have second thoughts. In his smooth understanding voice, he said, "I guess I just had a feeling and knew I wanted to be prepared. And I wanted you to be prepared so you wouldn't miss out."

Nowadays, when I tell him this story, dementia prevents his clear recall, but he smiles that same smile every time. He had prepared, long before that day, so that everything would be taken care of, because of who he was, and the relationship he wanted with his daughter. He knew that, even with my young aspirations of adventure, he was going to make certain that this escapade would be better than I had even imagined.

Jesus encourages (even warns) us to prepare "But concerning that day and hour no one knows, not even the angels of heaven, nor the Son, but the Father only" (Matt. 24:36). Even Jesus himself doesn't know the day that "heaven and earth will pass away." (Matt. 24:35) so he tells us "Therefore you also must be ready, for the Son of Man is coming at an hour you do not expect" (Matt. 24:44).

It may sound like a bit of a tongue twister, but we have a responsibility to prepare for the place that is being prepared for us. Preparedness begins by getting back to the basics and having faith to hear what we need to do. Romans 10:17 tells us "So faith comes from hearing, and hearing through the word of Christ." It begins with hearing the words of the one who is making it all possible. Hearing is only the beginning. James tells us in James 1:22, "But be doers of the word, and not hearers only, deceiving yourselves," and we are later told that "...a doer who acts, he will be blessed in his doing." (Jas. 1:25b).

This decision of faith continues with repentance and turning our eyes from Satan's goal of destruction to focus on the one who is constructing a place for eternal life. As we read from Luke 13:3, Jesus tells us "...unless you repent, you will all likewise perish." Once we repent and turn our eyes toward Jesus, we openly declare our faith with confession of our belief that Jesus Christ is the son of God. And once confession has been made, we demonstrate our faith by putting on Christ as we "...Rise and be baptized and wash away [our] sins, calling on his name" (Acts 22:16).

WRAPPING IT UP

Former French Emperor Napoleon Bonaparte is credited with the quote, "Most people fail because they give up what they want the most for what they want in the moment." Tim Lewis, in his book *The Domino Effect*, says that Napoleon's statement "explains why so many Christians fail to make good decisions. They give up what they want more for what they want in the moment. They give up heaven for the momentary pleasures of life here and now."

Mark 10:17-27 tells the story of a young man who ran up to Jesus, knelt before him and asked what he needed to do to inherit eternal life. This young man had been keeping the ten commandments all his life. Jesus told him one more thing to do. Jesus wanted him to be one of his followers, so he told him to sell everything he had and give to the poor and he would have treasure in heaven. Jesus saw his potential. Yet, this young man walked away from Jesus because he had "great possessions." Sadly, the last thing we know about this young man is that he gave up what he wanted most for what he wanted in the moment.

God is preparing a place for us, so "let us not grow weary of doing good, for in due season we will reap, if we do not give up" (Gal. 6:9).

Heaven is being prepared for us. God has been preparing this eternal city since the fall of Adam. There will be no need for the sun for the Lamb is the lamp.. There will be no night. God gives the light. We will have all we need, with no end. For this reason, let us set our sights on heaven!

There will be a noticeable absence of things we do not need —mainly tears, death, mourning, crying, or pain. God, himself, will wipe away every tear. Our tears will be wiped away by our Father, who is dwelling with us, and having the relationship he has wanted ever since he created man. For this reason, let us set our sights on heaven!

We want our children to be prepared for success in school by studying for tests, getting a good night's sleep, and being on time. We want our older children to be prepared for life after school, so we give them responsibilities because we want them to be able to do their best and achieve success. In fact, most people have done well to prepare for the world's expectations. But, how are we preparing for eternity? If the Lord specifically says that he is preparing a place for us and that he will come again, it would make eternal sense to set our eyes on Jesus and spend our time on earth getting ready for heaven and even help those around us be prepared. For this reason, let us set our sights on heaven!

QUESTIONS

1. List ways in which knowing that God is preparing a place for you in heaven encourages you to prepare for it.

2. What do the statements in Revelation 21:4-5 that "the former things have passed away" and "I am making all things new" mean to Christians?

3. After deeper study of God's preparation and longing to have a face-to-face relationship with his people, how has your understanding of God's compassion changed?

4. Think back to the quote from Napolean Bonaparte: "Most people fail because they give up what they want the most for what they want in the moment." What do people struggle with in today's world that causes them to give up what they want the most?

5. How does it feel to know that God himself is going to wipe away every tear from every loss you've experienced, and that he is preparing a place for you and is looking forward to having an eternal relationship with you? Write your thoughts on what that is going to be like for you.

BIBLIOGRAPHY

Clements, John R. "In the Land of Fadeless Day." <https://hymnary.org/text/in_the_land_of_fadeless_day>.

Hardman, W. LL.D., *The End of Pain.* <https://biblehub.com/sermons/auth/hardman/the_end_of_sorrow.htm>.

Lewis, Tim. *The Domino Effect: Changing Your Life One Decision at a Time.* Nashville: Gospel Advocate, 2015.

Lister, Thomas Mosie. "When We All Get to Heaven." <https://hymnary.org/text/sing_the_wondrous_love_of_jesus_sing_his>.

Millard, Bart. "I Can Only Imagine." <https://www.lyrics.com/lyriclf/466926/MercyMe/I+Can+Only+Imagine>.

Rambo, Dottie. "Remind Me Dear Lord." *Lyrics.com.* STANDS4 LLC, 2023. Web. 1 Nov. 2023. <https://www.lyrics.com/lyric/6871243/Connie+Smith/Remind+Me+Dear+Lord>.

Revelation 21—A New Heavens, a New Earth, and a New Jerusalem. <https://enduringword.com/bible-commentary/revelation-21/>.

Spurgeon, Charles Haddon. "Commentary on Revelation 21". *Spurgeon's Verse Expositions of the Bible.* <https://www.studylight.org/commentaries/eng/spe/revelation-21.html. 2011>.

Cayron Mann is a Licensed Professional Counselor and Ladies event speaker from Muscle Shoals, Alabama. She and FHU alumni Pam Lenz and Ben Hayes own and operate Three Cord Counseling (threecordshoals.com) where she is a certified EMDR therapist.

Before joining Three Cord Counseling, she owned a private counseling practice for eight years, as well as, serving with Renewed Spirits, a non-profit that offers equine-assisted therapy and The Healing Place, a non-profit children's grief center.

Widowed in 2010, Cayron learned first-hand the benefits and healing that can be found in receiving mental health therapy during bereavement. Because of this experience, and in honoring the life of her husband (Sam), she made it a goal to travel a path of helping others in their emotional struggles.

She has an amazing son, Cam, who is a senior at FHU, majoring in Christian Apologetics and Ministry and will graduate in May, 2024.

Because He is Coming Back, I Must Live Each Day for Him

Revelation 22

Lisa Beene

For those of you who love to read, you may relate to the feeling of anticipation as you get to the end of a great book. Some of you know what it is like to stay up much later than you should because you must know how the book ends. There is just something compelling about endings. How true this is of God's book. As we reach Revelation 22, not only do we reach the end of the great book of Revelation, but we also reach the end of the entire Bible. And what an amazing ending it is -- it is a reassuring reminder that because of the triumph of the Lamb over evil, the lives of faithful Christians do not end once we draw our last breath on this earth, but continue eternally. It is a reminder that because of the triumph of the Lamb, we must continuously reflect on our lives here and live each day for him.

Revelation is a book full of vivid imagery of beasts, dragons, sea creatures, of ferocious battles with evil; at times using symbolic language that appears strange and mysterious. With all these extraordinary images in earlier chapters of Revelation, there are many spectacular ways Jesus could have ended his revelation. How comforting it is that when we reach the final chapter, the focus is no longer just on the strange and mysterious, but on Jesus' love and concern for us and how we live our lives. In many important respects Revelation 22 is a final set of instructions and reminders of how the choices we make each day impact our eternity. Let's focus our attention on five of these final reminders from Chapter 22: (1) a reminder that heaven is our goal, (2) a reminder of the confidence we have in God's word, (3) a reminder to worship God, (4) a reminder that Jesus is coming back, and (5) a reminder of the urgency of sharing God's word with others.

A REMINDER THAT HEAVEN IS OUR GOAL
(REVELATION 22:1-5)

It is often said that to get successfully to your destination, you must begin with the goal in mind. How true that is of life's journey. If heaven is our goal, we must live our life each day with that goal in mind. We must keep our mind focused on the fact that heaven is a place specifically prepared for the faithful. In his earlier letter, John comforted the faithful by reminding them that they should not be troubled because Jesus was going to prepare a place for them in heaven (John 14:1-3). In Revelation Chapter 21, John begins his description of the New Jerusalem by painting a beautiful word picture of the exterior of the heavenly city—the city four-square, with foundations of precious gemstones, streets of gold, and gates made of gigantic pearls.

In Chapter 22, verses 1-5, he continues with a description that focuses more on the interior of the heavenly city: the great street of the city, the river that flows from the throne of God and the Lamb, and the tree of life (cf. Gen. 2:9, Gen. 3:22). The descriptions of the ever-flowing pure water and abundant fresh fruit in every season must have really captured the attention of the recipients of the letter in Asia Minor since they lived in such a hot, dry region where fresh water was sometimes scarce, and fruit was very limited at certain times. The description of pure water not only encourages the reader to reflect on the physical nature of water to sustain life, but on the spiritual nature of "living water" that will sustain the faithful for eternity (John 4:13-14). John then adds the description of the magnificent tree and notes that the leaves of the tree will be used for the faithful's healing.   Scholars believe the Greek word here is better translated with the idea of *nurturing* or *enhancing well-being* as opposed to healing from disease or injury, since there will be no disease or injury in our eternal home. What a comforting reminder that the Source of Life continuously provides for all our needs and our best existence.

John also reminds us that God is the Source of Light. There is no need for light in the holy city, because "the Lord God will be their light" (Rev. 22:5). [All scripture references are from the English Standard Version unless otherwise noted.] It is hard for us today with electricity so readily available, to imagine how important light was to people in the time Revelation was written. How exciting it must have been to hear that they no longer had to worry about light. We are also reminded that in the Bible, light is often contrasted with the darkness of sin. Verse 3 states that "No longer will there be anything accursed." The curse of sin is gone. There will be nothing to block out the radiant light of the Lord God. In heaven there will be no fears about what dangers the darkness of sin holds because the righteous will continuously have illumination provided by the Source of Light. The Lord of Light has indeed triumphed over the Prince of Darkness!

The verses in this section also provide insights on the forever relationships that the faithful will have in their heavenly home. Not only will there be wonderful reunions with cherished family members and friends, but also with the faithful from many nations and from many epochs of time. John's words spur us to imagine the joys of worshipping God with the faithful of all the ages and with all the heavenly beings. Together in unity the faithful will worship and serve God.

But of all the cherished relationships in heaven, the most precious relationship the faithful will experience throughout eternity is our relationship with God! John states, "they will see his face and his name will be on their foreheads" (Rev. 22:4). We know that no human throughout history has ever seen the face of God (Exod.

33:20, 23). How incredible to think that in heaven we will see God face to face! This passage also contains the reassurance of knowing that the faithful *belong* to Him – they wear his name. How glorious it will be in heaven to actualize the words from the beautiful old hymn, "Face to face shall I behold Him, far beyond the starry sky. Face to face in all His glory, I shall see Him by and by."

A REMINDER OF THE CONFIDENCE WE HAVE IN GOD'S WORD (REVELATION 22:6)

John may have anticipated that some would have trouble accepting the messages in Revelation. In verse 6 he asserts that "these words are trustworthy and true." Just because something is confusing or difficult to interpret does not mean we should question the validity of God's word or choose to ignore certain sections of it. It does not mean that we should expect additional revelations in the future to provide more information or further clarity. How many people have missed the message and the blessings of the book of Revelation because they have labeled it as "too difficult"?

As we reach the last chapter of the Bible, it is interesting to note the thread that runs from the first chapter of Genesis to the last chapter of Revelation. From the events in the opening chapter of Genesis to the time of Revelation approximately 4,000 years have passed and there have been approximately 40 different writers of the Bible. In all these years with all these writers, we see that God has revealed his word to man so that they will know his expectations as to how to live. As we read the closing chapter of the Bible with references to events thousands of years before, we see the continuity and internal consistency of God's word. We can believe in God's word!

In verses 18 and 19, John warns that no one should add to or take away from these words of Revelation. Even though this warning applies specifically to Revelation, we know there are other places in scripture where the same directive is applied to God's entire word (Deut. 4:2; Prov. 30:5-6; Matt. 5:17-19). It is sad that the book of Revelation has been so frequently used to promote error. We specifically think of how many people have been deceived by false teachings based on the second coming of Christ and premillennial ideas. Through the years many people have tried to convince their followers that they have had new and additional revelations from God. John speaks to the fate of people who add to or take away from God's word, "I warn everyone who hears the words of the prophecy of this: if anyone adds to them, God will add to him the plagues described in this book, and if anyone takes away from the words of the book of this prophecy, God will take away his share in the tree of life and in the holy city, which are described in this book" (Rev. 22:18-19). John reassures us that we can have confidence that we have God's word and that his word is truth!

A REMINDER TO WORSHIP GOD
(REVELATION 22:3, 9)

In verses 8-11 there is an interesting exchange between John and the angel who is showing him the visions. John appears to have been so overwhelmed by the marvelous visions that he "fell down to worship at the feet of the angel." At this point, the angel rather emphatically instructs him *not* to worship him, but to worship God. He reminds John that God alone is deserving of our worship, love, and reverence. This was a critical message to the people of that day when there was so much emphasis on emperor worship. In fact, one of the reasons John had been exiled to Patmos was due to the Roman officials' fear that John would lead people away from emperor worship to worship God. John is reminding Christians in Asia Minor of the importance of being faithful and worshipping God even in the face of intense persecution. He encourages them to remember the rewards that await the faithful.

In this last chapter of Revelation, John reminds his readers of the awesome nature of the God we worship. His omnipotence is reflected in the triumph over Satan. His omnipresence is reflected in his presence throughout time--past, present, and future. Living in the presence of God throughout eternity is clearly emphasized. His omniscience is reflected in his knowledge of the hearts and minds of all mankind throughout history. Because he is all knowing, he can fairly judge the deeds of men and determine if their names are written in the Lamb's book of life (Jer. 17:10; Rom. 2:6; 1 Pet. 1:17).

There is an important reminder in these verses for the people of our day not to get so caught up in the cares of life that we forget to worship God. We must constantly examine our priorities and the things in our lives that interfere with our worship. In this closing chapter of the Bible, John gives us at least three reminders of the rewards of remaining faithful to God and putting God first in our lives. In verse 5 he reminds us that the rewards of the faithful are forever—"they (the faithful) will reign forever and ever." In verse 12, he reminds us that our rewards are based on our actions on this earth—"Behold I am coming soon, bringing my recompense with me, to repay each one for what he has done." In verse 14, he reminds us that the faithful will enter the heavenly city—"Blessed are those who wash their robes, so that they may have the right to the tree of life and they may enter the city by the gates." What amazing rewards await the faithful!

A REMINDER THAT JESUS IS COMING BACK
(REVELATION 22: 7, 12, 17, 20)

"I am coming!" Jesus reminds readers four different times in this chapter that he will return to this world. In three of the four verses he adds that he is coming *soon*. Jesus is coming back to take the faithful to the beautiful place he has prepared for them in heaven. This closing chapter emphasizes that Jesus has not forgotten us and abandoned us to a world of sin and evil, but that he is coming back and that he will take the faithful home.

There has been much discussion through the years over the word "soon." Some have even suggested this as evidence that Revelation cannot be authentic because Jesus has not returned in a time frame they consider to be *soon*. We should remember that God's timetable is not our timetable. Second Peter 3:8-9 states, "But do not overlook this one fact, beloved, that with the Lord one day is a thousand years, and a thousand years as one day. The Lord is not slow to fulfill his promise as some count slowness, but is patient toward you not wishing that any should perish, but that all should reach repentance." We should appreciate that Jesus' definition of *soon* allows us to get our own lives in order and to reach as many others as we can. We must not, however, develop a false security that lulls us into complacency. We must be prepared for his coming at *any* time. First Thessalonians 5:1-2 reminds us, "Now concerning the times and the seasons brother, you have no need to have anything written to you. For you yourselves are fully aware that the day of the Lord will come like a thief in the night." Matthew 24:36 reminds us, "But concerning that day and hour no one knows, not even the angels of heaven, nor the Son, but the Father only." How we live every day is our preparation. How we live each day makes a difference in where we will spend eternity (2 Pet. 3:11-18). Are we ready like John to say, "Come, Lord Jesus?"

Revelation assures us that God is a God of love, who repeatedly invites his children to *come* to him. But Revelation also assures us that God is a God of *justice*. "Behold, I am coming soon, bringing my recompense with me, to repay each one for what he has done" (Rev. 22:12). We are accountable for how we live our lives, and our eternal destiny is at stake. Just as John's words in Revelation paint a strikingly beautiful picture of heaven, they also paint a strikingly horrific picture of hell. These last verses in the book of Revelation are a sobering reminder that we must obey God's word and daily examine our priorities. We do not know *when* Jesus will return, but we know that he *will* return (Matt. 24:36). We must be ready. We must live for him each day.

A REMINDER OF THE URGENCY OF SHARING GOD'S WORD WITH OTHERS (REVELATION 22: 10)

Revelation 22 reminds us that many are lost in sin and will not share in the wonderful rewards of heaven described in this chapter. John does not mince words; he clearly states that there are consequences for our life choices and that some will not enter heaven. In verse 15 he specifically states, "Outside are the dogs and sorcerers and the sexually immoral and murderers and idolaters, and everyone who loves and practices falsehood." John gives the sobering reminder that there are people who are lost and who need us to share God's word with them. In verses 11 and 12, he emphasizes that time is of the utmost importance, and that there will come a time when it is too late to repent. John writes, "Let the evildoer still do evil, and the filthy still be filthy, and the righteous still do right, and the holy still be holy. Behold, I am coming soon, bringing my recompense with me, to repay everyone for what he has done."

Our goal should be not only to make heaven our home, but to take as many people as we can with us. John is specifically told "do not seal up the words of the prophecy of this book." (Rev. 22:10). It is important that people have access to God's word and knowledge of what they must do to be saved. We must remind others that only Jesus saves (Acts 4:12). We must share the great redemption plan that began in Genesis when *paradise was lost* due to the entrance of sin, that is now wonderfully concluded in Revelation with the description of *paradise gained*. We must remind people of God's love, mercy, and grace and that he *invites* all to come to him. He wants us to live eternally with him. The time for sharing the good news about salvation is urgent — "the time is near." (Rev. 22:10). The outcome of the decisions we make regarding time is critical to where we spend eternity. If our decisions cause us to miss heaven, we miss everything.

CONCLUSION

What a blessing the book of Revelation is! Just as John promised in the very first chapter, those who study the book of Revelation are blessed with insights that they would never have had otherwise. They are blessed with deeper understanding of the truths of God's words and what God expects of his followers. They are blessed with amazing descriptions of the splendors of heaven. It is hard to read

John's magnificent descriptions of the heavenly city in the last two chapters of Revelation without humming the lines of so many beloved hymns that have inspired the faithful for generations. Oh, how beautiful heaven must be!

Those who read and study the book of Revelation are blessed with some critical reminders, for Revelation is a book of reminders. We are reminded of an all-powerful God who created us in his image. We are reminded of a God that loves and provides for his people from the Garden of Eden through eternity. We are reminded that he sent his son to redeem his people from sin. We are reminded of the great promise that Jesus guides us through the difficulties of each day. We are reminded of the hope, comfort, and encouragement that we can have in his great promises. We are reminded of his repeated invitation to come to him. We are reminded of the beautiful home in heaven where the faithful will live eternally with God and the redeemed of all ages. We are reminded that because Jesus is coming back to take the faithful home to heaven, that we must live each day for him!

QUESTIONS

1. What other "practical lessons" could be added to the list from Revelation 22? What other "practical lessons" could be added from other chapters in Revelation?

2. What songs and hymns do you think of when you read Revelation 22? Are there particular lines/verses that impact your understanding of what heaven will be like? What are your favorites?

3. List the names, phrases, and titles that are given to God and Jesus in Revelation 22. How do these descriptions enhance our understanding of the nature of God and Jesus.

4. What keeps us from reaching out to those we know have fallen away from their obedience to God's will? How should we approach conversations with them?

5. What keeps us from studying the book of Revelation? What are the "blessings" that come from studying Revelation?

6. What are the promises in the book of Revelation? How do these promises impact the way you live your life?

BIBLIOGRAPHY

Bragg, David. *The Sunset of Scripture. Hope and Promise From the Isle of Patmos: A Interpretation of Revelation*. Henderson: Hester, 2007.

Couch, Mal. *A Bible Handbook to Revelation*. Grand Rapids: Kregel, 2001.

Elwell, Walter A. and Robert W. Yarbrough. *Encountering the New Testament: A Historical and Theological Survey*. 2nd Ed. Grand Rapids: Baker 2005.

Motyer, Gutherie and Stibbs Wiseman. *The New Bible Commentary: Revised*. Grand Rapids: Eerdmans, 1970.

Mounce, Robert H. *The Book of Revelation*. 2nd ed. Grand Rapids: Eerdmans, 1998.

Pack, Frank. *The Message of the Book of Revelation*. Volume II. Hester, 1984.

Tsarfati, A. and R. Yohn. *Revealing Revelation: How God's Plans for the Future can Change Your Life Now*. Eugene: Harvest, 2022.

 **Lisa Beene** is a native of Henderson, Tennessee. She and her husband Sammy live on a family farm in Chester County. They are the parents of Jacob and Lauren and have one grandchild, Brayden. They worship with the Henderson church of Christ. Lisa has taught children's Bible classes there for over thirty years.

Lisa serves as the chair of the Department of Behavioral Sciences at Freed-Hardeman University. Her primary teaching responsibilities are in the Social Work program. She is a Licensed Clinical Social Worker.

58094419R00134